Forced Focus

First published in 2007
© Penny Burke

The National Library of Australia Cataloguing-in-Publication:

Burke, Penny, 1966- .
  Forced focus: the essence of employer branding.
  1st edition
  Includes index.
  ISBN 9780977577309.
  ISBN 0 9775773 0 9.

  1. Personnel management. 2. Marketing - Management.
  3. Organisational effectiveness. I. Title. 658.3

Project Management: Messenger Publishing Pty Ltd
www.messengerpublishing.com.au
Editing: Geoff Whyte
Book printed in China by Bookbuilders

Messenger
Marketing

Forced Focus

the essence of attracting and retaining the best people

Penny Burke

Preface by David Blackley

It wasn't so much that Penny Burke arrived at Clemenger BBDO, Melbourne, twelve years ago, it was more that she hit the place like a typhoon.

She was young, forthright, energetic and very, very enquiring.

From the outset she kept putting her head around my door to ask strings of questions or to make observations on our business. She was never a nuisance; in fact her questions constantly made me think and reassess - Penny just had to know how this particular marketing communications organisation worked, what it believed, why it believed it, and which techniques it used in going about its craft etc. etc.

It soon became obvious to everyone, clients included, that Penny was not only fiercely intelligent, but she loved applying her intellect and boundless enthusiasm to solving marketing challenges – with an end result of adding significant value to clients' brands. In a nutshell, Penny is a born marketeer – and her evangelism tends to carry all before it.

During her decade at Clemenger BBDO, Penny (at various times), held many of the company's most senior positions in Strategy, Research, and Account Management – and she was a board member in both Melbourne and Sydney. However, her first love was always marketing strategy, and I am so pleased that she has written this book on her favourite subject.

I should admit here that I am not a fan of many business books. I tend to find them glib and gimmicky and, in the end, of limited practical value.

Not so *Forced Focus*.

This book, with great clarity, tackles the critically important subject of how a company should position and market itself to its own employees – a subject that can only become more vital over the decades ahead as the shortage of skilled talent escalates.

Penny takes the reader step-by-step through the processes involved, and explains the straightforward techniques that can be applied to bring success. At the end of the book there are fascinating case studies from a diverse group of companies.

I firmly believe that if companies were to take on board the lessons of *Forced Focus* they would be far better companies, with improved management understanding and more motivated employees.

And there could be no stronger recommendation than that.

David Blackley,
Former National Creative Director and Chairman of Clemenger BBDO, Melbourne.

Dedication

For the four wonderful men in my life:
Darcy and Max, my best friend Trev, and Charlie

Contents

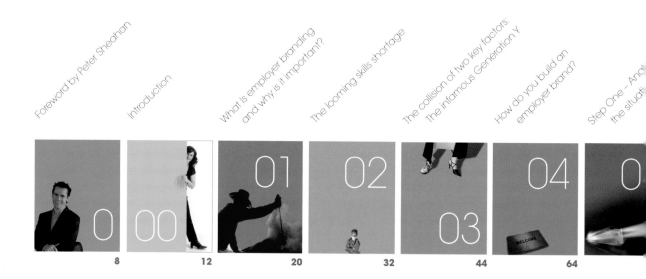

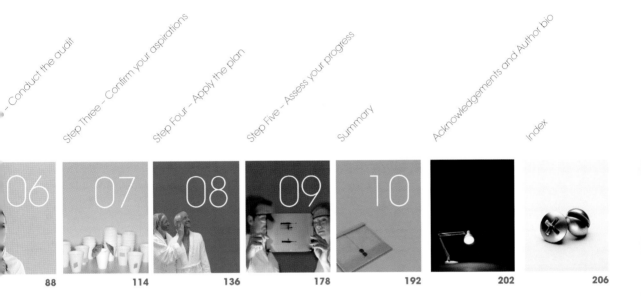

Foreword by Peter Sheahan

I first had the pleasure of working with Penny on a Ministerial Review of Australian Defence Force Recruiting and Retention, and was deeply impressed by her understanding of marketing and communication. What impressed me the most, however, was her ability to apply the expertise she had gained working in advertising for some of Australia's leading brands to the internal employee experience.

Penny flips the notion of branding as being something we do externally on its head, and suggests we apply the same principles internally. Using relevant market information, international data and local examples, she makes a compelling case for building better internal brands – that is, proactively selling (and indeed developing) the virtues of your employment 'product', both to the people who are already working for you, and those who you would like to attract.

There could not be a better time for business to hear and heed this message. The skills shortages and supply challenges we are currently experiencing in the labour market are unlikely to improve in the short

to medium term. In fact, they're going to get worse – much worse, I suspect.

The net result of these worsening factors will be a continued shift in power from the organisation to the talented individual. Remember the good old days, when you used to interview the candidate? Is this the case today? Hardly. It's more likely that the candidate is now interviewing you or, as one of my clients pointed out to me last week, interrogating you: 'Are you people-friendly? What is your work–life balance policy? What have you done about that? Do you have balance in your life? What about corporate social responsibility? Do I get time off work to pursue philanthropic activities? What charities does the business support?' And on it goes.

Individuals have so much more choice now: where to work, when to work. And they know their market value. As you continually attempt to create increasingly mind-blowing experiences for your consumers and clients, you need better and brighter individuals who can create those experiences. You need talented people who can generate the innovative thinking you require to obtain and maintain your competitive edge. And, as you know only too well, as a result of the ageing workforce, high employment levels and other assorted market factors, they aren't exactly lining up in droves, and are increasingly willing to move on when they feel their work is done, regardless of whether you agree.

This is not just a generational issue either. As Penny and I suggest, Generation Y are definitely screaming out for more inspiring and inclusive workplaces, but I suggest to you that everyone else is as well. Perhaps the only difference is that Gen Y is more likely to leave an organisation, or at the very least to voice their concern when they are not happy with the status quo. Penny outlines succinctly what she believes talented people want from the workplace and anecdotally, I think she is spot on – not just for Gen Y, but for people right across the age spectrum.

In reality, the major opportunity open to organisations today and in the coming years is the mature workforce, as opposed to Gen Y. However, all the research I have read to date suggests that the Baby Boomers and Late Builder generations will want some wholesale changes to the way they participate in the workforce if they are to be retained.

Penny manages to apply the principles of marketing to the internal employee as 'customer' (and I suggest that as employers, we are increasingly going to need to think of our staff as customers, and treat them with the same respect we extend to our external customers), and does so without bombarding the reader with buzz and hype. The material is delivered in Penny's characteristic punchy, direct and frequently humorous style.

In many ways, this book is a call to action – a call to leaders of organisations, large and small, to deliver on their promises. The compounding factors of a tightening labour market, rising customer and client expectations and more demanding employees are 'forcing' organisations to focus on marketing themselves as attractive places to work. They need to make good their promises about 'what it is like to work here', and to show that they really do understand that 'our people are our most important asset'.

Enjoy the ride ...

Peter Sheahan

Introduction by Penny Burke

I don't often have lightning-like flashes of inspiration, which is what made the one I had early in 2005 so unusual.

I have always been fascinated by the psychology of why people buy what they buy. How does one determine which margarine is best? What brand of toothpaste is for you? What shampoo will suit your hair? When a person switches from one brand to another, particularly after an extended period of loyalty to a particular brand, what makes them do that? Did they have a disappointing experience? Was another option cheaper? Did they just get bored?

Marketing and brand behaviour and, in particular, advertising – the pointy end of marketing in many respects – was always going to be my destiny. I've been lucky enough to be involved with some of Australia's most successful advertising campaigns: from Pro Hart and his Stainmaster carpet, to the frisky retired milkman and his 'Legendary Stuff'; from historic brand stalwarts such as Sorbent toilet paper to helping build emerging brands of the 1990s like Uncle Tobys. Through it all, I have always been obsessed with brand behaviour and the changing nature of brands and markets that make marketing an ongoing enterprise. For more than twenty years, I have studied markets, analysed trends, and prepared clients for future market changes, focusing on why people buy what they buy.

On this particular day, I was sitting in the reception area of one of my clients, reading their newly created vision that was proudly posted in the foyer for all to see. Clearly, management felt a company vision for the future was in order, and they had created this marvellous mission statement with an accompanying set of values that expounded claims such as 'we value our people', 'we act with integrity', 'we partner our customers' and 'we are good corporate citizens'.

It was gazing at this poster, and recalling the many I had seen in a range of other companies saying basically the same thing, that made me realise that this 'sell' of the workplace to potential (and existing) employees was akin to how sophisticated brand marketers talk about their products to consumers. 'We act with integrity' and 'we value our people' is the workplace equivalent of 'superior comfort' or 'best tasting'. And while traditional marketing companies spend lots of money ensuring they do in fact engage with their customers appropriately with their list of benefits, it dawned on me that very few employers do the same thing. Whereas the marketing department spends considerable time and money fine-tuning the external brand in minute detail, the representation of the internal brand isn't afforded the same luxury.

Similarly (some would say consequently), from the 'customer' perspective, it appears employees are not as connected to, or as engaged with, their employment brand as they are with the goods and services they are able to purchase as a direct result of that employment. The workplace is where many of us spend at least five days every week (often more time than we spend with our life partner), the place to which our aspirations and ability to progress in life are inextricably linked, and where for many our self-esteem and sense of self is determined. Should we not be as emotionally attached to that place as we are to our Nikes?

And shouldn't employers want their staff to be every bit as involved and engaged as their most loyal customers? Do employers really believe that whacking a poster saying 'we act with integrity' and so forth in the foyer of the office is the most powerful way to achieve that engagement?

The lightning bolt had me wondering if employers felt that they needn't bother treating their staff the same way they treated their customers, that maybe they didn't consider them to be as important as paying customers.

Not deliberately, mind you, I think many CEOs believe what they say when they expound the virtues of their staff. It's just that, often, what they think versus how they behave gets lost in translation. Let's face it, for years employers have been able to stumble along, treating their workers with veritable contempt, in some cases, as if it were a privilege to work at the organisation with no apparent downside. And, in turn, many staff did indeed see work as a privilege.

Well, that's about to change. The research upon which this book is based suggests the market is changing and the power is shifting, just like it has at many other times in history, in many other markets. For example, remember the good old days of shopping around for your first home loan, and how demeaning that process was? You practically had to beg the bank manager to lend you the money, demonstrating that you were a fine upstanding citizen, and would willingly hand over your first-born child should there be a hiccup with the repayments. All the power was with the banks. Now, one merely has to whisper 'home loan' out of the corner of one's mouth and a battalion of personal sales consultants armed with laptops and colour spreadsheets materialises on your doorstep after dinner, or 'at a time that suits you, sir or madam, to discuss how we can tailor a loan to suit your particular needs'.

What on earth happened there? Why is it suddenly difficult to attract and retain great staff? How and why do markets change so significantly?

Choice is what happened.

Fundamentally, choice forces a shift in power from the seller to the buyer, the pertinent word being 'force'. Now I don't actually recall the banks coming out and actively leading the charge to be more flexible and customer-friendly. The fact is, they were forced to change (in order to maintain their market share by competitors) who had begun to offer choice to consumers.

The same is true with airlines. I don't think Qantas had ever offered a $100 fare in their history, not even when $100 bought a whole lot more than it does today, until Virgin arrived on the Australian scene. Then they were forced to, in order to compete. Of course, demand can force prices up as well as down, depending on the scarcity and perceived value of the resource – witness world oil prices.

This is not an attempt to start a debate on the virtues or otherwise of a free market economy, or on the value of competitive trade practices. Rather, it is the result of these fundamentals of economic behaviour that I find interesting.

A good brand is not one that makes consumers feel good about the brand ...

Where choice explodes, and power shifts to the customer, it forces changes in markets. Market changes open up windows of opportunity for brands, which compete to engage customers through their brand offer. People are the very essence of brands. My all-time favourite quote on brands comes from legendary Australian social researcher Hugh Mackay; 'A good brand is not one that makes consumers feel good about the brand. A good brand makes consumers feel good about themselves'.

Darn right. And the workplace is no different. Substantial change is coming in the world of employment, and it promises to be every bit as important as other fundamental shifts that have revolutionised the workplace, irrevocably changing the nature of engagement.

Yet the concept of a 'brand' in the workplace is embryonic! The lightning bolt that hit me in reception highlighted the irony that, despite the diminishing power of the employer and the overwhelming need for the employer brand to communicate effectively with both current and prospective employees, the workplace brand is one of the most under-utilised areas of brand development.

There's no reason why a workplace shouldn't be considered as a brand, one that strives to make its employees feel good about themselves.

Marketers have long understood this nexus – that consumers make decisions about the brands they align with on both rational and emotional grounds. Their engagement is about so much more than just the functional attributes a product offers. The emotional engagement a brand promises is vital. Clearly, a product or service has to stack up in the logical sense, and satisfy a customer need. Even the best advertising campaign can't sell a tractor to someone living in a block of flats. Good brands, however, do much more. They meet an emotional need that may not be entirely logical. My brand decisions are decisions about me – my life, my choices, the kind of person

A good brand makes consumers feel good about themselves

Hugh Mackay

I am and would like to be, my values. Just ask my husband, who continues to buy classic gas-guzzling, V8-powered cars as fuel prices continue to climb, despite our financial position, because 'new cars are boring'. His choice of car is far from rational, but it defines him.

It is in markets that have undergone dramatic change where choice has exploded, that brands fight for engagement like seagulls over a potato chip. This is where 'Forced Focus' becomes paramount. This is the focus – brought about by force – necessary to make your brand offer as relevant as possible, in order to maintain your market share.

There seems to be little doubt that the employment market is ripe for 'Forced Focus'. The concurrent factors of a looming global skills shortage, and the significantly different attitudes towards work of emerging generations (such as the infamous Generation Y), will force a power shift away from employers towards employees. The emergence of 'Forced Focus' will fundamentally change the current rules of engagement.

The marketing focus of most companies revolves around refining the brand promise to consumers in order to maximise engagement and generate loyalty towards the brand. The entire marketing effort is directed outwards, towards the products or services a company sells. There is a distinct lack of corresponding effort aimed at promoting the company brand internally in order to engage and develop the loyalty of current or potential employees.

Of those companies who do seek to promote their corporate brand to engage internal markets, many limit their efforts to the functional aspects of their offer. Despite knowing that the real key to the external success of their brand is not the functional attributes but the emotional appeal of their brand to consumers, when it comes to their internal audience, many explain their offer in terms of base-level hygiene factors.

'Forced Focus' seeks to simplify the often complicated world of marketing and branding

The degree of preparedness for the coming global revolution in corporate labour management and ensuing employer brand development differs all over the world. Some countries, such as the United States, are well down the track of understanding the impact of good corporate branding, although even there the concept is still in its infancy. In Australia, we are significantly off the pace. Many companies are blissfully unaware, some are aware but haven't got the faintest idea how to address the issue, and only a very small proportion are taking positive steps to better manage their future.

This book has been written to help employers hone the brand focus that will inevitably be forced upon them. It navigates the entire experience of employer branding, explains why it is important, and demonstrates how to develop your employer brand. It contains case studies and tools so employers can think about their brand and their future themselves, without resorting to expensive consultants to help them through the process. It showcases some examples of what other companies are doing well, and not so well, both in Australia and globally. This book is the result of many months of international research with employers and employees, and is one of the first of its kind in Australia.

Above all else, 'Forced Focus' seeks to simplify the often complicated world of marketing and branding. After all,

the very essence of a good brand is clarity of promise, so a consumer knows exactly what they are buying. This is no different whether we are talking about a brand of product, a brand of service, a brand of industrial component or a brand of employment.

You have the power to unite your most important asset in the pursuit of your organisation's goals, and this book demonstrates how to do now what will ultimately be forced upon you. Take the opportunity to focus – it has never been more important to do so.

I hope this book helps you in your endeavours. Good luck!

01

01

What is employer branding and why is it important?

Employer branding is not a new phenomenon. Dr Noel Purcell, Westpac's Group General Manager, Stakeholder Communications, speaking at a Strategic Communication Management Summit in 2004, told how Westpac's front-of-house employees would head to the loo at the end of each day to change out of their uniforms before leaving, due to the level of angst that was being directed their way because of the public outrage over what banks were doing at the time. Such actions have a pervasive effect on a person's sense of self.

There are plenty of jobs that do not engender cosy feelings of warmth and gratitude, for example parking inspectors. Not everyone can be a nurse or teacher, or something else that evokes positive feelings, but there is generally a very real separation and distinction between the job you do and the company you work for.

It's one thing to be part of an organisation that people avoid doing business with, but it's another thing entirely to actually feel ashamed of being part of an organisation's brand. The behaviour of those Westpac employees was a clear reflection of how they felt about the company they worked for, and it was their action that galvanised management to review their brand promise, both internally and externally. In a simple demonstration of the power of getting it right, once Westpac overhauled their internal brand management, they were actually able to sell (at a staff discount of course!) branded t-shirts to a willing internal market who were now proud to be wearing the brand of their employer.

Employer branding is the perception employees (both current and potential) have of the promise by the employer. It incorporates reputation, core competency, and culture – all the fundamental aspects that distinguish and shape the overall brand promise of any other brand.

And as with any other brand, if there is a disconnect between what the brand promises and what the brand delivers, the result is a disillusioned customer base.

Attracting and retaining the best people is becoming a real source of competitive advantage

There is a rule of thumb in marketing circles that for every customer who complains about an unsatisfactory interaction with the brand, there are probably another eight who are equally unhappy, but you never hear about them because, rather than complaining, they just quietly abandon your brand.

Imagine that situation in an employer brand setting. If, for each employee who complained about the organisation and then left, you knew there were eight more who were equally disillusioned with their employer brand, and were probably on the verge of doing the same, given half an opportunity, that would result in some 'Forced Focus'! Customers are more likely than ever before to complain loudly and bitterly about their interactions with brands, and employer brands are no different. We're already starting to see signs of this, and there will be more on the key factors that have led to this situation in the next two chapters.

I recently visited notgoodenough.org to peruse the latest list of brands that customers felt had not lived up to their promise. Among the usual litany of product gripes, one user's story stood out. They wrote of their experience applying for a job with a home loan provider (home loans again!) through a recruitment consulting group:

'The job ad specified good customer service skills, flexible attitude, etc. The job was for a home loan specialist, no experience needed. The agency offered me the job on a Friday, and I was to start the following Thursday.'

It transpired that after the offer was made, the recruitment agency retracted the offer of employment on the grounds that the employee had no previous home loan experience, in direct contravention of the condition specified in the advertisement, which the agency then changed. Meanwhile, the poor individual involved had already turned down another job offer in order to take this one, and was now left without a job at all, not to mention some very strong, unpleasant feelings towards not only the recruitment agency, but the company offering the job – strong enough to post their discontent for all the world to see on notgoodenough.org.

Now companies, like people, make mistakes, and this may well have been an innocent one. But one of the marks of a strong brand is how well they manage the complaint process. Many brands actually emerge in better shape following a corporate crisis. Witness the strength of the Snickers and Mars brands following the blackmail attempt involving threats to poison products in Australia in 2005. Despite a massive and costly product recall, a process of timely, clear and honest communication to the public enabled both brands to rebound strongly. If people believe in the brand promise, they will also forgive the occasional mistake or service upheaval. The issue is one of trust.

So why should a company develop a more robust employer brand?

The 'unfair share'

A more robust employer brand will enable you to attract and, equally importantly, retain your 'unfair share' of the best people. Many companies parrot statements such as 'we view our people as our greatest asset', but most demonstrate by their behaviour that this is not in fact the case. In a global market where skills shortages are starting to bite, attracting and retaining the best people is becoming a real source of competitive advantage.

An engaged workforce

Arguably the most critical reason for

developing a strong employer brand is to deepen the nature of the relationship you have with your employees, by creating emotional engagement. In the traditional marketing world of products and services, reference is often made to the differences between a habitual purchaser and a loyal one. A habitual purchaser buys your brand week in, week out, because that's what they've always done. They don't think about it, they don't really consider other alternatives, they're content. But it's a habit. Until one day, they stroll down the aisle and discover another brand on special. Or perhaps it has an offer attached – a chance to win something maybe. And they think well, why not? I've always used brand X, but maybe it's time to give brand Y a go.

This is the moment of truth for many brands, because it exposes the fact that the customer you always thought was loyal was not actually engaged with you on an emotional level at all. They just bought your brand out of habit. This is what employers need to avoid. It will do you and your company no good at all to have a workforce made up entirely of habitual employees. You need them to actively choose to work for you, to want to work for you.

One of the foibles of human nature is the perception that the grass is greener on the other side of the fence. Many employees are presented with opportunities elsewhere and,

if your workers are merely habitual, they will be more open to change. If you have loyal employees, they are more likely to collaborate with you in negotiating alternatives to leaving. A strong employer brand increases the emotional engagement employees have with the company.

CEO of Visa Australia, Bruce Mansfield, understands this inherently, and sums up the key focus of his efforts in the area of building an effective employer brand in one word – engagement. 'Are your employees engaged and happy is fundamentally what we are talking about', he says. 'They can be happy and they can be busy and doing whatever they do, but they may not be engaged … the outcomes are clearly much more productive if they are. You can have a completely disengaged workforce that has no desire to leave the organisation, but they just come in and do what they need to do to turn the wheels every day … at Visa, we want an engaged workforce.'

Marcus Blackmore, CEO of the healthcare products company Blackmores, simplifies what he pursues in his workforce even further – happy workers. His mantra is 'People, Product and Passion', but if he had to name his most important pursuit it would be a happy workforce. 'If you make people happy they work harder, they enjoy their work and they are more productive', he says.

The United States-based Walker Loyalty Report looks at precisely this issue. The 2005 report, which was the fourth in the series, claims there is considerable advantage in converting employees who are merely satisfied into those who

> One of the foibles of human nature is the perception that the grass is greener on the other side of the fence

are truly loyal. Although 75 percent of American employees say they are satisfied, only 34 percent are rated as truly loyal (as defined by classifying themselves as committed and planning to stay with their current employer for at least the next two years).

Nearly 60 percent of the American workforce see themselves as either trapped (they have no choice but to stay) or high risk (plan to leave inside the next two years). More important than the statistics is the finding that loyalty affects behaviour. The Walker report claims that 95 percent of truly loyal employees will recommend their company as a good place to work, compared to 35 percent of the trapped or high risk employees. Similarly, 95 percent of the truly loyal said they go above and beyond the call of duty, compared with 62 percent of those who lack loyalty.

On a global scale, market research company Synovate conducted a study in Bulgaria, the Czech Republic, France, Hong Kong, Hungary, Romania, Russia, Singapore and the Ukraine early in 2006.

The Synovate *In:fact* study found that overall, 40 percent of employees think it's no longer possible to be as loyal to a company as in the past. French workers led the way, with 56 percent of respondents echoing this sentiment. Larry Crosby, CEO of Synovate's Loyalty Practice, commented that 'While a certain amount of turnover is to be expected, excessive voluntary turnover hurts the bottom line. The total cost of replacing an employee can run five times their annual compensation. Companies around the world are being challenged to keep their best employees while attracting new talent, and this is driving considerable interest in programs designed to strengthen the employer – employee bond'.

An effective workforce

So how much more effective is a workforce with a strong bond than one without?

Gallup surveys around the world in 2002 and 2003 yielded some interesting statistics in this regard. The 2002 United States survey reported that less than a quarter of workers were fully engaged, at an estimated annual cost to the economy of some US$300 billion. British Surveys undertaken in 2003 produced similar findings, with more than

80 percent of Britons reported to be lacking commitment to their job. Looking at such factors as employee retention, absentee levels and productivity, Gallup estimated that disengaged workers were costing the British economy up to £38 billion annually.

In France, the 2003 survey results indicated that 31 percent of workers were disengaged, and only 12 percent were positively engaged in their work. And in Singapore, the rate of disengagement was found to be on the increase, with 17 percent of workers now disengaged, up from 12 percent in 2002.

Similarly, James Wiggins, APAC Head of Employer Branding of global firm TMP Worldwide's employer branding division, points to research that he says provides empirical evidence that organisations with committed employees provide shareholders with a return on investment (ROI) six times that of organisations with low employee commitment. Further, those firms with effective internal communications delivered shareholders an ROI twice that of those whose internal communications were deemed to be ineffective.

It's important to understand that it's not just a matter of getting the functional aspects right. It might seem logical that the guy in the corner office on the 52nd floor with a sweeping view would be highly engaged and much more effective than the guy doing the dirty job out on site, but

this is not necessarily the case. Studies have shown engagement to be more dependent on the way the individual is managed within the workplace culture than on the functional aspects of the job he or she undertakes. This is why the notion of 'Forced Focus' in developing an employer brand is so important, because it is not just about what is functional – the 'what' of doing business – but also very much about the way we engage the workforce – the 'how'.

A 2001 Maritz poll in the United States noted that 49 percent of American workers indicated that the company brand or image played a key role in their decision to apply for a job at a particular organisation. Clearly, this is a global issue which, together with developing worldwide skills shortages, augurs for a challenging future in relation to the recruitment and retention of high-quality personnel. Importantly, it's not just warm fuzzy feelings that employers compromise by not maintaining strong engagement with their employees – it's cold hard measures of productivity, bottom line results and ROI, that suffer.

So, how are we doing in Australia?

Specialist recruitment company, Hays, recently undertook some research to determine attitudes towards employers in Australia and New Zealand. The results highlighted the importance of reputation management. It is telling that a staggering 86 percent of candidates were not prepared to work for a company with a bad reputation, even if they offered a higher salary than one with a better reputation.

This attitude was further highlighted by research I conducted among Year 12 and tertiary students and young workers who had been in the workforce for less than 18 months. Factors such as reputation and image figured prominently in their choice of employer, with one 18-year-old respondent stating that 'The perfect company has got to have moral fibre'.

Moral fibre? I don't think I've ever heard an 18-year-old comment on the moral fibre of a company before, but there's plenty who talk in terms of 'corporate social responsibility' and 'being ethically involved in the community'. Another commented that 'If it is an immediately recognisable company, and it is well respected in its field, that grand image is usually enough to make people go, oh well, I will go for that one ...'

Perhaps I shouldn't have been surprised because, after all, the youth of today are the masters of brand engagement, understanding inherently that when they buy into a brand, they get much more than just what the functional offer is – they get a badge, a lifestyle, a personality!

The first law of leadership

Ries and Trout, in their famous book *The 22 Immutable Laws of Marketing*, state that the first law of leadership is 'It's better to be first than it is to be better'. At present, employer brands are not seen as strong forces. Nancy Woltzen, Vice President for VersantWorks, stated in 2004 that in her view, 'less than 10 percent of US organisations currently have true employer brand programs in place'.

In Australia, one would expect the statistics to be similar. The first employer in each category to build and execute a truly employee-focused brand will reap the benefits of an empowered, engaged workforce. Attracting and retaining more than your fair share of quality employees in a slowing market is more than just a sensible proposition – it is a key competitive driver and tool that will allow you to maintain or grow market share and maximise profitability.

Keep your eye on the ball

The fourth reason for building a strong employer brand is to keep you and your senior management focused on your people. You may well be reading this thinking your company has no problem. Your reputation is excellent, and all your employees think so. If that's the case, I'd be saying, 'Are you sure?'

Another leading global recruitment firm, Hudson, released a report in February 2006 that revealed the findings of research involving more than 8000 Australian employers. Frighteningly, it reported that most Australian businesses believed that they were a good employer with a positive work environment, but when these responses were compared with employee attitudes, a significant disconnect emerged. According to the Hudson report, 80 percent of Australian business managers considered their employer brand to be proactively managed, clearly understood, and aligned with employee expectations, but only half of these employers were using formal monitoring tools to actively measure and evaluate their reputation as an employer. One can't help but wonder how, then, they can be so sure of their status.

In a separate study, also conducted by Hudson, some 63 percent of the 2500 Australian workers surveyed reported that the employment experience promoted to them turned out to be inconsistent with what they actually experienced. Again, this reflected a major disconnect between the employers' views of their brand and their brand as experienced by employees.

Degree of best fit

The final reason why an employer should develop a strong employer brand is to improve the ability of the company to attract, hire and retain employees who are the 'right' cultural fit.

In the world of consumer marketing, it is often said that it is better to stand for something than to stand for nothing at all, and yet some brands, in a desperate attempt to appeal to anyone and everyone, end up appealing to no-one. People want to know what a brand

actually stands for, so they can determine whether or not it is aligned with their belief system and values. Brands that are closely aligned with a person's belief system stand to forge a much stronger connection with that person, thereby creating a loyal customer, rather than a habitual one. Brands that have a clean slate (i.e. that do not stand for anything in particular) generally have less loyal customers, because it's hard to find something for them to hold on to, or believe in.

One of the great conundrums of branding is that the best thing about a clearly-defined brand is that people know what it stands for – and the worst thing about a clearly defined brand is that people know what it stands for!

I will talk more in later chapters about just how important the notion of culture is to employees but, for now, suffice to say culture can be hard to define. The research I undertook for this book led me to spend time sitting in the reception areas of more than 30 organisations around Australia while I waited to interview CEOs and senior management, and I can tell you that every workplace has a distinct culture, which is evident right from the reception area. Even an environment that appears devoid of culture will be defined by that culture, albeit weak or

insipid. Generally, a company that has a distinctive internal brand is in a better position than one with a less defined culture, since a distinctive culture makes it easier for both parties to determine if you're the best fit for each other.

The best talent does not always equate to the best cultural fit. One company I used to work for had a very strong internal culture that took me some time to get used to. When I discussed this with senior management, it was explained to me that there was a recognised 12-month 'breaking-in' period for new employees to become acquainted with the culture. Management saw a pattern where, in the first 12 months, new employees would struggle to come to terms with the culture, and then one of two things would happen. They would either succumb and be happy working there for life, or they would leave. The internal culture was so strong that it weeded out the 'misfits' and disposed of them during the first 12 months.

The Managing Director of Cardinal Health in Australia, Ronda Jacobs, said the same thing – that fit is important. She has taken the company through somewhat of a restructuring process in the 18 months since she took over the role: 'Do I still have people who aren't a good fit and how much damage is that going to do to me and to them … You can ruin really good people and they can ruin you when you haven't got that right'. Rich Field, Brand General Manager at Virgin Mobile, discovered the same thing when he left Virgin to go to Coca Cola to launch Zero. He relished the opportunity to be involved in such an amazing project, but found that Coke, despite having a strong sense of external brand, did not have a specific internal culture that was a reflection of their external brand: 'Coke is like that – you either love it, a lot of people have been there forever … or you go no, not for me'.

Now this is not all bad. As I said, it is better for a company to stand for something than to stand for nothing at all. Given that the need for talented workers is going to increase in the future, a well-defined employer brand will serve to unite all employees in a common belief system. The more clearly defined the culture, the easier it is to recruit people who can thrive and grow with you. Of course, companies need to guard against a culture of robots where everyone approaches challenges in exactly the same way. But a strong culture, managed correctly, can return big dividends to employers, and one sign of a strong culture is an equally strong employer brand.

ING Direct, the direct banking company, have taken this one step further, and have a number of cultural values in their business. Sharyn Schultz, their Executive Director of HR, explains that culture is so integral to the ING Direct business that 'we recruit first on culture and then we recruit on technical skills'. The values are strongly aligned internally and externally to the point where they drive the internal culture, and create a better place to work.

All these factors emerge from the application of 'Forced Focus'. It makes sense to start building an employer brand if you haven't already done so, otherwise it will be forced upon you. Start to focus on it now, and you will be ahead of the game. Your employer brand is what your company stands for, your DNA, your promise, the very essence of what you are about. Present your brand to existing and potential employees in such a way they can understand and identify with what you offer, and you stand to gain more than your fair share of the talent pool, thereby obtaining competitive advantage, and maximising your company's chance of success.

After all, value – be it shareholder or company value – is not created by the company itself, but by the people who populate the company.

02

02 The looming skills shortage

So why has employer branding become the buzz term of the moment? Whenever a market undergoes fundamental change, that change is often forced by external factors. Companies don't suddenly decide that they want to improve their branding – they are forced to address the issue by the emergence of new market factors.

There are two key factors emerging in relation to the employer market. Firstly, the growing shortage of employees, commonly referred to as the skills shortage, and secondly, the changing attitudes towards work and work–life balance of emerging employees, most notably the infamous Generation Y. This chapter focuses on the skills shortage debate and predictions of future labour force patterns, while the following chapter summarises the findings of my research into Gen Y and their attitudes towards work.

Are we facing a global skills shortage?

There is plenty of debate about whether or not the world is in fact facing a skills shortage. I do not intend to mount an economic argument about the factors underpinning world employment and labour force planning – I'll leave that to the economists. However, given that a labour shortage will have a palpable effect on attracting, hiring and retaining the best quality staff, it is worth making some attempt to contextualise the facts in a digestible manner.

In no particular order, here are some pretty startling statistics in relation to the global labour market:

- In 2013, 50 percent of the world's workforce will be in India or China, and by 2025 these two countries will produce 27 percent of world GNP (World Bank).

- Between 2000 and 2010, the population of Europe will decline by over 14 million.

- By 2030, the European Union's active labour force will be 20 million short of the levels requiredto sustain growth and pay for an ageing population.

- The US Bureau of Labor Statistics projects a shortfall of 10 million workers in the US by 2010.

Whichever way we look at them, these observations indicate a fundamental shift in world labour markets. For a start, never before have we had 50 percent of the world's workforce in just two countries. Clearly, the fundamental demographic change characterised by an ageing population worldwide is having a significant effect on the availability of talent. In some industry categories, there is already such a shortage of specific skills that it is restricting the economic growth of both industrialised and developing nations. As the labour hire company Manpower noted in their White Paper

In the near future, for almost certainly the first time in history, more Australians will leave the workforce than will enter it

on the issue, 'A demographic crunch is coming, which will be exacerbated by a talent crunch that threatens to stall the very engines of that economic growth'. In a further attempt to quantify the emerging talent shortage around the world, Manpower recently conducted a survey of nearly 33,000 employers in 23 countries. Overall, they found that 40 percent of employers worldwide are having difficulty filling positions due to the lack of availability of suitable talent. Mexico, Canada and Japan were the countries doing it toughest, while India was the least problematic.

While debate may rage about the actual effect of shortages on the global economy, the research indicates that we will almost certainly experience a critical shortage of skilled staff in many key fields, and many businesses may well fail as a result of not planning ahead to deal with this talent shortage. Significantly, the signs also suggest that the shortage will not be merely cyclical, as may have been the case in the past. At best, this looming problem is likely to last for decades, but given the decline in birth rates in so many countries, it could be here to stay.

Australia is mirroring world trends in relation to labour force issues. In the Manpower survey referred to earlier, the top ten job categories that employers are having difficulty filling in Australia are:

1. Sales Representatives

2. Engineers

3. Skilled trades (primarily welders, boilermakers and plumbers)

4. Accountants

5. Technicians (primarily production/ operations, engineering or maintenance)

6. Drivers

7. Mechanics

8. Receptionists

9. Administrative assistants and PAs

10. IT staff

This is a close reflection of worldwide trends. Consider also the state of our national labour market. In June 2006, the unemployment rate in Australia fell to 4.9 percent, the lowest figure ever recorded, and the unemployment rate among 15 to 19-year-olds who were looking for work (and therefore arguably entering the labour market for the first time) was even lower, at 4.5 percent. It is clear that, as at June 2006, Australia was enjoying conditions of low unemployment and relative economic buoyancy.

However, it is predicted that over the next few years, more Australians will leave the workforce than will enter it. This has major implications for employers.

Of Australia's current workforce of just over 10 million people, 70 percent are 45 years of age or older. Over half of these workers intend to retire (the others say they are happy working, or will be forced by economic necessity to work on, but inevitably at a reduced level of intensity) and the trend has increasingly been for them to retire earlier than they predicted. This looming wave of retirement will leave a significant, and in certain employment categories catastrophic, hole in the labour market.

Related projections don't look any brighter, either. Australia's civilian labour force aged 15 and over is projected to grow to 10.8 million in 2016, an increase of 1.5 million or 16 percent from the 1998 figure of 9.3 million. Yet the overall participation rate is projected to decline, in part due to the ageing population. The labour force is projected to age dramatically, with over 80 percent of the projected growth occurring in the 45 years and over group.

There are currently four workers for every retiree, but by 2042, there will be only three workers for every two retirees. The CEO view on this situation appears to be mixed. Greg McKibbin, CEO of Kodak in Australia, said that 'At this stage we are not necessarily noticing a skills shortage'. Paul Thompson and Peter Sinclair from SCA opine that the skills shortage in New Zealand is more noticeable than in Australia. Ronda Jacobs, MD at Cardinal Health, says specific areas such as Research and Development are suffering massive shortages. And Doug Shears from ICM says, 'We have been suffering a shortage of skills from the ground up for about five or six years and predicting that it would get worse, as now appears to be happening … those CEOs who say

there are no shortages, I would say they must be paying well above the odds'.

In summary, Australia shows no sign of bucking the international trend. Given this bleak outlook, global labour market pundits predict that a number of patterns will develop in response to the looming skills shortage. Given the overwhelming demographic changes and declining birth rates in some countries, one of two things is likely to happen: either work will move to where the people are (aided by technology), or people will move to where the work is.

Moving the people to the work

The concept of moving to where there is work is not exactly a new phenomenon – the difference now is that it's a buyer's market, not a seller's. The countries with the fastest growing populations are often also the poorest, so it is reasonable to expect that we will see an increase in the export of human capital from these countries, and a corresponding increase in imports by resource-starved developing economies. Countries such as Spain, Italy and Greece face urgent demands in certain skill categories, and have already begun the push for skilled immigrants, particularly from the Balkans.

Asian countries such as Japan are actively attracting substantial numbers of workers from the Philippines, Indonesia, China, Thailand and Pakistan. The United States, having spent so much time and energy trying to keep Mexicans on their own side of the border in the past, may now decide that welcoming them with open arms is a better economic proposition.

Of course for countries like China and India, the trick will be luring their human capital back to power their own development rather than just being a provider of cheap labour for other countries.

In Australia, we have already turned to immigration as a source of labour. In 2004–05 our population increased by 110,000 through immigration, which accounted for 46 percent of the total population growth for the year. However, these levels are nowhere near enough to meet the growing demand for skilled workers. The Australian Bureau of Statistics (ABS) notes that despite the growth in the labour market in Australia, the participation rate is projected to decrease. If immigration continues at current levels, it is unlikely to be large enough to prevent

work will move to where the people are ... or people will move to where the work is

a significant fall in the rate of employment growth compared with that which we have experienced in recent times.

For example, to achieve a 1.8 percent increase in employment each year, Australia's net immigration would need to increase from current annual levels of around 100,000 to 280,000 by 2016.

The ABS looks at three separate assumption cases when preparing future immigration projections, but even the most optimistic assumption case predicts annual net immigration reaching no more than 140,000 by 2007, and remaining constant thereafter.

Moving the work to the people

The corollary of moving the people to the work is of course moving the work to the people. Technology is the emerging facilitator of more flexible work practices (check out elance.com, a site I have used to post projects and attract a global workforce). As Thomas Friedman notes in his book *The World is Flat*, 'It is now possible for more people than ever to collaborate and compete in real time with more other people on more different kinds of work from more different corners of the planet and on a more equal footing than at any previous time in the history of the world, using computers, e-mail, fibre-optic networks, teleconferencing and dynamic new software'.

Friedman cites outsourcing as one of the ten forces that has flattened the world and, by way of example, quotes the outsourcing of the preparation of US tax returns. In 2003, 25,000 returns were outsourced to India. By 2004 it had grown to 100,000 and in 2005 it was 400,000. Similarly, my Editor has clients in the US who send documents through electronically at the end of the day and then, when they log in the next morning, hey presto, there's the document all edited and ready to publish – 24/7 operations and no postage expenses!

The practice of moving the work to the people is obviously facilitated by technology, but also reflects another new and growing form of flexibility – the growth of part-time and casual work, a trend we are already seeing in Australia.

Between 1971 and 2001, the proportion of employed persons working full-time declined from 89 percent to 69 percent. At the same time, we saw a similar growth in the service sector, but many of those new jobs were part-time. By 2003, 26 percent of employees were part-time, up from 22 percent in 1993.

This increase is seen as a double-edged sword, however. There are many Australian workers who have no doubt enjoyed greater flexibility in terms of their work-life balance that the availability of part-time work offers, and yet the ABS suspects that many part-time workers would in fact prefer to be working more hours, and are therefore effectively underemployed. This group includes young people, single parents, people with disabilities, and older people trying to supplement their pension. In September 2005, the ABS determined that 6 percent of our 10 million strong workforce was underemployed, and 91 percent of those workers were part-time. If we are looking for a solution to the problem of finding more people to do the work, it seems clear that greater utilisation of the underemployed element of the workforce provides an obvious opportunity.

Another form of flexibility is represented by people who work full time, but in a freelance capacity. In the United States, the number of people who freelance,

work on a contract or temporary basis, act as independent consultants or are business-owning entrepreneurs make up 22 percent of the total workforce. We are seeing a similar trend towards self-employment in Australia as the use of freelancers and contractors continues to grow. Small business is on the march in Australia, with an 81 percent increase in the number of small businesses between 1984 and 2001.

In terms of employment, the small business sector recorded an increase of 66 percent over that period, an average annual rate of 3 percent. At the same time, employment for businesses other than those classified as small increased by 52 percent, an average annual rate of 2.5 percent. This is suggests a transformation in the labour force away from employment in big organisations.

According to research from The Career Innovation (Ci) Group, based in Oxford, UK, the trend away from big business has a lot to do with frustration. In their 'Manifesto for the New Agile Workplace' survey of over 2,000 people from 32 countries, Ci found that almost half (45 percent) are what they termed 'flexers' or 'agile performers'. These are people who are looking for more flexible arrangements and new ways of working, and are leaving their place of employment to find it. Over half

Flexibility is also about 24/7 workplaces

(55 percent) of all respondents rated a complete change of direction as attractive, with 'working for yourself' universally nominated as the most popular employment option.

Increasing flexibility is also evidenced by the growth of the virtual office. It is estimated that by 2010, more than half of the US workforce will spend more than two days a week working outside the office (Sulzer Infrastructure Services, UK). With ongoing developments in technology, it is already easier than ever to work remotely. It is estimated that there are currently around 28 million 'teleworkers' in the United States.

Flexibility is also about 24/7 workplaces. Circadian Technologies estimates that some 24 million US employees work at night, as companies attempt to increase their business base. While the traditional shift-worker role may remain, labour force analysts predict a growth in flexible working hours in highly-skilled roles in response to the increasing need to converse with the rest of the world in real time.

Of course, countries like India are well and truly there with their telemarketing facilities. Competition for jobs of this nature in India is fierce, because not only do they pay well, but you get to study during the day and work at night, providing one of the key stepping stones to an improved standard of living. The impact of this in a worldwide sense will cause some rethinking, not the least of which is management of the family home and the need for night-time babysitters.

In the future, we may well see a pattern whereby more and more workers are managing their own destiny and moving in and out of traditional corporate positions with increased freedom and satisfaction. Big business will be forced to focus.

A move back to training

A shift towards increased training is one clear way to overcome the skills shortage, although not many governments are keen to embrace it, given the massive cost. And it does need to be a government-led policy, because it starts in schools, with educational and vocational training.

China is investing in improving English language skills in order to prepare its workforce for a global onslaught. In Mexico, government policy is aimed at improving access to education and raising standards in schools. Other countries need to follow suit.

Having said that it needs to be led by government, it can't remain the exclusive domain of governments. Employers need to do their bit with enhanced on-the-job training, and this is arguably where the biggest shift needs to occur. At least governments regard training in schools as part of their core service, but not enough corporations share that view. Training is often not budgeted

for, undertaken in an ad hoc and unmeasured fashion, or simply paid lip service in a busy corporate life. Employers need to mandate training, and to see it as part of their commitment to their people and, ultimately, their external audiences. Call it 'Forced Focus' training!

All parties need to get creative in terms of how training is delivered. New technology provides some wonderful opportunities for training to be delivered in a streamlined, economical and effective manner. Some companies are already going offshore and establishing strategic alliances with learning institutions, or even setting up their own training units in foreign countries in order to be at the start of the wave of importing human resources. There is a vast range of technologies and programs that could be tailored towards, for example, people with a disability, to enable more effective engagement of this underemployed group, and provide a more energised future workforce. In particular, given the ageing population, there is large potential upside in recruiting and re-skilling the 'grey army'.

Finally, it is important that training and skill-building is seen as a lifelong

undertaking. The skilling up of a workforce for the future is not something that can be done once and then assumed to be complete. The skills people possess when they enter the workforce should not be the only ones they exit with. 'Continuous improvement' has long been the catchcry of corporations seeking to improve their customer focus. Now they need to bring that focus inwards.

In Australia, we appear to display a disturbing disinterest in training, both in the government and corporate sectors. Overall, training appears to have lapsed into a pattern of periodic ad hoc commitment, reflecting a very short-term view of the looming talent shortage. For some of the critical categories listed earlier, the only way out is through a commitment to ongoing training, particularly for the more specialised jobs.

Yet fewer and fewer government apprenticeships are being made available, although the government would argue that there is a broader base of different types of schemes. The Foundation for Young Australians notes that since 1993 there has been a decline in the number of traditional apprenticeships. Since the early 1990s the training rate has declined by 16 percent, with the major industries affected being metal trades (down 19 percent), electrical trades (down 23 percent) and building trades (down 15 percent).

Training has become more expensive to deliver, and the increasing reliance on contract labour and outsourcing has resulted in lower levels of on-the-job training, a classic example of short-term thinking. As a recent OECD paper commented, 'Productivity improvement comes from combining technology and skilled human capital. Job opportunities for the unskilled and poorly-educated are shrinking almost everywhere'. If this is not a call to arms for greater training, upskilling, and reskilling, I don't know what is.

Greater diversity

Diversity is not a new concept, especially in a multicultural country like Australia, but it stands to reason that the workforce of the future MUST be more diverse than the one of the past. I am referring here to much more than ethnic diversity, despite this being an obvious area of focus if we wish to increase our net immigration rate in order to keep growing the labour market. Ethnic diversity is certainly important, but there are several other minority groups that could be targeted to enable greater participation in the workforce of the future.

Manpower make another bold statement in their White Paper referred to earlier: 'Fifteen years after the American Disabilities Act took effect, only one-third of disabled Americans are employed, even though more than two thirds of unemployed people with disabilities say they would like to work (D&I Workers with Disabilities)'.

People with disabilities may be an emerging minority group, but what of another long-term disadvantaged group – women? Now I'm no bra-burner, but it does seem outrageously unfair that, despite female workforce participation climbing to the highest ever rate of 45 percent, and 56 percent of university graduates being female, women still only hold less than 9 percent of ASX Board Director positions. Of the Boards of the 200 companies that comprise the ASX200, women only hold two Chairs of Boards and four CEO positions. If this is an example of the diversity that the nation has spoken about and celebrated for some years, the practical reality is that, in the workplace, the change has barely registered. It appears we have been merely paying lip service to the concept of diversity.

The key is to look at labour force options in a more creative fashion. Global charity Oxfam is moving away from traditional job descriptions and using a combination of full-time, part-time and contract workers to design the best team for the job, so it is starting to happen. What is inarguable is that the skills shortage will make its presence felt in the Australian economy in the future. One way or another, we will be forced to focus on the growing need to attract and retain top quality staff in a market that is declining.

This shift puts more power into the hands of employees, which is a fundamental change in the labour market dynamic. For too long, employers have held an inordinate share of the power, displaying almost an 'ask not what your company can do for you, but what you can do for your company' mentality. Well, the signs suggest that those days are over.

For the first time, as happens in any other crowded market filled with aggressive competitors, and where demand increasingly exceeds supply, company brands will need to fight it out for their audiences' favours. They will need to demonstrate why they should be considered. They will need to earn the respect of their people, rather than assuming that it is their right, and they will need to present much more than just functional attributes in their offer if they want to attract and retain a loyal following.

The effects of a skills shortage will see the emergence of some very different patterns in the labour force of the future, which is why employer branding will become so much more important to Australian companies.

03

03 The infamous Generation Y

I am not of the school of thought that believes generational change is necessarily cataclysmic, and that each generation comes through with astounding differences that characterise them as completely different to anyone who went before them (or after for that matter). However, it is certainly evident that people learn their behaviours from the values of their parents, and are influenced by the way they are brought up. This, together with the impact of their peers, defines the normative social behaviour of their tribe. This results in shared characteristics that can and do reflect certain attitudes and dimensions of various generations. In short, I definitely believe that people are a product of their parents, but they are also a product of their environment, and it is the marriage of these elements that gives rise to generational characteristics.

But first, how do generations distinguish themselves? We've all heard of Baby Boomers, those born between 1946 and 1964. In 2006 the first of the Boomers will turn 60, and they continue to influence the Australian landscape, if for no other reason than that there are so many of them! As Bernard Salt says, 'It is a demographic avalanche after a demographic desert'. Their sheer numbers outweigh those of the generations who, living through the war period, preceded them.

The generation following the Baby Boomers, those born between 1965 and 1979, are known as Generation X. Gen Xs are commonly regarded as the cynical generation, observing the aftermath of delirious materialism that Boomers celebrated, but yet to actually enjoy any of the benefits of their labour. In fact, Gen X are the only generation

> In order that people may be happy in their work, these three things are needed: they must be fit for it. They must not do too much of it. And they must have a sense of success in it
>
> John Ruskin 1819 – 1900

in history to have lived through not just one recession but two, so it's little wonder they are characterised as a cautious, negative bunch whose credo is 'work hard and do what you can to assure your future, because the future is more likely to be difficult than prosperous'.

And then we have Generation Y, those born between 1980 and 1995. There are around four million Gen Ys in Australia, and they will become the bulk of the adult population in the future and the backbone of Australia's workforce. This group is starting to demonstrate some specific attitudes towards the world of work that, together with the skills shortage, will force a seismic shift in the workplace. Much of my research centred on this cohort, and they're a pretty interesting bunch. Their attitude towards life represents some confronting behaviours, particularly for Gen Xs, who display a natural mix of pessimism and optimism. Some of the key attitudes that Gen Ys demonstrate towards the workplace carry startling implications.

Two views on the difference work makes

It is not entirely true to say that for the generations that preceded Gen Y work was their number one priority. But certainly, the recessions that Gen X lived through, and the well-known materialism that Boomers displayed, and continue to display, have led to a much greater focus on the relationship between working for financial reward and family and life goals. Work still represents the opportunity to build a secure future for all generations, and Gen Y is no exception in this regard, but their interpretation of what security means, and how to obtain it, appears to be changing.

Somewhere between the corporate downsizing of the 70s and 80s and the growing prevalence of terrorism and uncertainty since the 90s, and particularly since 9/11, the natural order of work in the life of a Gen Y changed.

There now appear to be two distinct groups forming in Gen Y in relation to work attitudes. They either want to work hard and make a difference, or they have decided that work makes no difference.

1. Wanting to make a difference

Within the group who want to make a difference, there appears to be a further sub-division into two emerging attitudinal segments – one that is altruistically driven, and one that is financially motivated.

For those Gen Ys driven by altruistic tendencies, the number who talk about work giving them an opportunity to make a difference is significant. Certainly for some, it is a search for meaning in their life. As the previous CEO of adidas pointed out to me, the definition of 'meaning' is based on how you are able to spend your time, not just how you are able to spend your money. But the quest for meaning and the desire to make a difference is not just some youthful, self-serving grandiose

plan to save the world. This is cold, hard, goal-setting underscored by the logic that says 'If I'm going to be doing this five days a week, then it better be worth something'.

For Gen Ys in this cohort, work is a driving force in their life, a trait that has led to the coining of the term 'occupassion' – witness the respondent mentioned earlier discussing the importance of the 'moral fibre' of companies. This group wants to know what workplaces are doing in terms of social responsibility. They want to feel good about where they work (what was that that Hugh Mackay said about how a good brand makes you feel?), and they want to feel good about themselves. This is their way of seeking security, wanting to feel sure about themselves and their future, by making a meaningful contribution.

When asked what they want out of their working life, the overwhelming majority say 'to make a difference'. As Katie, 19, said, 'You would like to feel you are valued, if not by the community, at least by yourself'.

Or Mark, 22: 'That you are not just there doing a job that could be done by anybody – that you are making a difference within your workplace, that you are contributing'.

And Noreen, 21: 'I think that what I would look for really is a sense of achievement, so that I come home from work and know I have done something productive, not to benefit humanity, but just so I know myself that I have done something'.

Which is all well and good, but if you can show me a job where I can benefit humanity and get paid a fortune, bring it on! This group shows all the thirst for success and ambition as your most voracious Boomer of the 80s. They are extremely materialistic, they want to climb the dizzy heights of 'careerdom', and they want it now.

They want to make a difference and climb the corporate ladder – but they also want to comfortably manage their burgeoning credit card debt, all without working long hours! Does that sound like a contradiction? You bet it is!

The second group of Gen Ys who say they want to 'make a difference' seem to want to do so for purely financial reasons, without the same passion for making a difference to society. While work may be their occupassion, it is clearly seen as a means to an end, not an end in itself. As the gap between the rich and the poor continues to widen in Australia, I have seen comments indicating that, for the first time ever, the poor know they are poor.

Gen Y knows there are two classes emerging, and they know which one they want to be a part of. For this group, it is a more traditional quest for security. I met one young man who was working three jobs (two his own business concepts) in order to amass a large enough real

estate portfolio to enable him to retire at 28 and live off his investments. He is clearly motivated at work, but his catchcry is definitely 'Show me the money!'

'The only reason I work is to take a financial step towards the next goal … and the next time a higher paying job comes along, I'll grab that and that's how I work. A job's a job.'

'I only work for a simple goal – like, my cost of living is low, so I will work for x amount of weeks to achieve that goal … I only work for specific short term goals.'

Work for a number of weeks, you say? My, that's commitment! This belies an absolute hunger for work – but not out of ambition to improve performance, to learn more or contribute to the company. It is about pursuit of one's own life goals and, as one girl pointed out, it's a never-ending search for betterment.

'I think you should never be happy at the level you are at really …'

2. Work makes no difference

Despite the continued commitment of those Gen Ys for whom work is about making a difference, there is a growing number of Gen Ys for whom work makes no difference to their lives. Again, this group of Gen Ys appear to be made up of two attitudinal sub-segments. First, there is the socially disadvantaged segment. As at June 2006, there were 257,000 unemployed people aged between 15 and 24, with one out of every seven young people looking for work. For them, financial recompense and security is what drives their work ethic. In truth, many of these Gen Ys actually reflect more of a Gen X attitude to work and life, such is the tenuous nature of their existence. They are the disenfranchised disengaged, for whom work means much the same as it did to their parents and grandparents before them – a means to an end.

The second segment of Gen Ys for whom work makes no difference demonstrate a far more radical attitude towards the nature of work. As a pair of 22-year-old respondents, both studying for their second degrees, confided to me:

'I just think work could be one of the least important things in my life … I don't want my life to be defined by my job. I want a good job, but I just don't want it to be the be-all and end-all for me.'

'I mean, it's just work, it's not your life.'

It's a refreshing attitude really – isn't that the pinnacle of what every Gen X says they want? To be in a position where work doesn't dominate your every waking moment, where you can focus on the things that are most important in life? How often do we actually make that happen?

Certainly, I made a decision to leave full-time employment after twenty years in the workforce. This decision was precipitated by the birth of my second son, the uncomfortable realisation that I was missing out on valuable time with both children and the sudden overwhelming need to get some perspective and find a better balance. Have I found that yet? Not really! Who starts their own business and is able to actually work less hours, not more? Not many! But at least now the hours are on my terms, not someone else's.

My sister commented to me the other day how difficult it continues to be to achieve work–life balance. Another Gen X, and now the CEO of a company, she had just been forced to take compassionate leave when her mother-in-law passed away. Three days after the funeral she had to fly to the US for a meeting. She didn't want to go, and her family didn't want her to go, but go she did, and felt pretty ordinary about it, too. She remarked ruefully, 'You say your family is the most important thing in your life, yet I go overseas at a time I'm really needed. Doesn't look like it, does it?' Gen Ys in this segment probably wouldn't have gone.

One Gen Y I spoke with had discovered, while doing teaching pracs as part of her Bachelor of Education course, that she didn't like the work at all.

'I just thought, I don't want to do this. If this is my job, it's just too much. Too much effort, I think. Even though that seems unambitious, I would rather put my ambitions into other things than work.'

Work–life balance, indeed.

But what of the economic implications of such decisions, I hear you ask? (I certainly did!) How do you intend to support yourselves? Buy a house? Live the wonderful life you lead once you get kicked out of the family nest? A Gen Y from Sydney responds:

'I don't care if I don't earn a lot of money. I'm used to living with no money, and that's a sacrifice I'm willing to make to have more of the life I want to have.'

This particular Gen Y is 24 and already living out of home, contrary to the trend. 'Ha', I hear you say, 'I used to feel like that when I was young too, didn't have a care in the world! Then I grew up, met my partner, and we settled down and bought the house, so we had to work'.

Ah yes, buying the house. Certainly that was one of the key factors that forced us all into settling down and committing ourselves to a life of work. But what if you didn't have a mortgage? While Gen Ys have enjoyed comfortable childhoods, the economic realities that hit them as they enter adulthood are significant. They are a highly educated group (the ABS notes that they stay in school longer, achieve higher

levels of education, and are more likely to participate in education beyond school), but they are increasingly burdened with extremely large HECS debts, and face skyrocketing housing prices, not to mention the ever-increasing cost of living.

The Annual Demographia International Housing Affordability Survey of 2006 identifies Australia as one of the least affordable housing markets in the world, with Sydney, Melbourne and Adelaide all ranked in the top (or should that be bottom?) 20 least affordable cities. The median house price in Australia is now equal to nine times average per capita income, compared to six times in the mid 1990s. It is little wonder then that according to CPA Australia, four in ten Gen Ys do not believe home ownership is achievable.

Similarly, statistics compiled by the Foundation for Young Australians (Susan Pitman et al., 2003, *Profile of Young Australians: Facts, Figures and Issues*) indicate that home ownership among young people is declining, while the likelihood of renting for longer periods is increasing.

This trend is undoubtedly partially driven by the highly tribal characteristics of Gen Y. They are extremely close to parents and peers, so geographic location is important to them. Consider a Gen Y, living in the middle-class suburb of Drummoyne in Sydney, wanting to buy their first home. It is common to find that

They don't go on what they are told - they go on what their gut tells them

their entire existence revolves around their environs, and yet affordability would be likely to drive them to the extreme outer suburbs of Sydney in pursuit of a home of their own. This is a move that many Gen Ys are simply unwilling to make.

'I have learnt to value other things in life … I would really like to have a balanced life with family and friends and work that I enjoy.'

So this group, who say that 'work makes no difference', do not reject the notion of working – it's just that they see that other things are more important. And they're not just saying it – they mean it and, as opposed to many Gen Xs who express a desire to live that way, these Gen Ys will actually do so.

Loyalty is dead

Despite not experiencing first-hand the two recessions that Gen Xs did, Gen Y observed from the sidelines and in so doing, formed some fairly assertive views about the nature of the workplace. Don't forget, this is a generation who may have grown up in a family where dad spent a considerable length of time climbing the corporate ladder at a large institution, only to have the world fall apart one day when he found himself out of a job, made redundant due to downsizing, a merger, outsourcing, changing job requirements, etc. Young people, old memories …

'From what I have heard and from what I have seen, loyalties might be different, but that's because we don't have the security any more. I might want to be in this job for 30 years, but these guys aren't going to say we want you in this job for 30 years.'

'Back then there seemed to be company loyalty, you start with a company, you stay with that company, you don't go to a competitor. Now I don't think we care that much about company loyalty.'

Many CEOs and senior managers look back on this period and agree that real damage was done. Shane Freeman, head of HR at ANZ says:

'If you go back through the 80s and 90s when everyone was adopting very economic rationalist models, it never quite delivered all the benefits and it certainly put the wind up workforces …
I think we probably screwed that up a bit.'

What is interesting is that the resultant expectations of Gen Y and the statements they make about loyalty are not said with any great sense of wistfulness. Gen Ys by and large do not yearn for the security of the old days – frankly, the idea of being in the same job for 30 years is horrifying. But they are savvy, optimistic and street smart. They talk the talk and give as good as they get. They don't go on what they are told – they go on what their gut tells them. They know the rules of engagement have changed.

'They expect loyalty from us, but they don't give it back.'

When I consulted the dictionary for the definition of loyalty, it said, 'true, faithful, to duty, love or obligation'. How interesting. The very essence of branding is about emotional connections that are made because people build a genuine bond with the brand. It is out of desire – not obligation. And that is where the workplace will come unstuck.

Workplace attitudes the world over continue to be more akin to the antiquated manufacturing-based models of the industrial revolution. These workplace support structures are outmoded and dysfunctional, yet they are still used to service a rapidly changing modern workforce. For too long, companies have taken advantage of the old-fashioned loyalty their employees offered them, and then let them down, rather than reciprocating.

I can't tell you the number of times I have heard CEOs expounding that 'people are our greatest asset', only to see them behave in precisely the opposite manner – or, as someone commented to me recently, exhibiting the corporate behaviour of 'sleazing up and bullying down.' As Boomers and Gen Xs, we accepted their shabby behaviour and slunk back to our offices, grateful that at least we weren't one of the unfortunate few who had been restructured out of a job. Gen Ys have learnt not to have high expectations of their employers. That way, they won't get disappointed.

'As far as mentality goes I think a lot of people go into a job assuming that at some stage they are either going to be laid off or they are going to jump ship.'

No fear, no hysteria, no outrage
– that's just the way it is. And
Gen Ys will behave accordingly.

'You don't care about the company, you
care about yourself, you are number one,
so if you're not happy you are going to
go somewhere else that can fulfil that.'

Which leads me to a point I touched
on earlier about the length of time
Gen Ys expect to stay at any one place of
employment. In the old days, we saw this as
a measure of loyalty. I can remember when
I was in my 20s, and in my first few months of
employment at a particular company, we
gathered together one afternoon to drink
champagne and toast the receptionist,
who had clocked up thirty years with the
organisation. I remember thinking 'Lordy, this
woman has been working here for longer than
I've been alive!' It seemed incomprehensible
to me, and that was over ten years ago, so
I can imagine how the Gen Ys feel today.
Incidentally, I went on to spend twelve years at
that company, so they must have been doing
something right to encourage such longevity!

But things are different now. You ask a
Gen Y how long they expect to stay in their
job, and their horizon is horrifyingly close …

'I would stay for two or three or five years
tops, applying for others while I am there.'

'Between one and three years … looking
for a better offer, a better chance.'

'To be honest, working for over one year
in the same job sounds horrendous …'

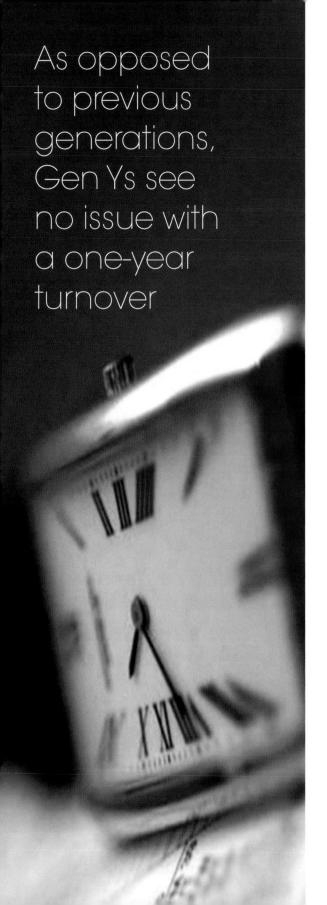

As opposed to previous generations, Gen Ys see no issue with a one-year turnover

Now I don't mean to be alarmist. I'm not saying for one moment that the entire workforce of the future will have a churn rate of one year, although there are plenty of studies around the world that suggest this may well be the case. The Synovate report referred to earlier found that one in four Russians and Ukrainians have changed jobs in the last year, almost twice as many as any other country surveyed, so it's not out of the question!

The point here is that, as opposed to previous generations, Gen Ys see no issue with a one-year turnover. It is not a sign of disloyalty, a lack of attention span, or an inability to knuckle down and do the hard yards, as Boomers may remonstrate – that's just how they are.

It is also incorrect to assume this changeability is purely related to salary or other working conditions. I interviewed a girl in remote central Australia who had spent many years pursuing her career as a chemical engineer. She had advised her workplace of her intention to leave, and they were devastated. Was she unhappy? Unfulfilled? Did she want more money? More social time? More responsibility? What did she want?

She wanted to try archaeology.

Archaeology? How was the employer supposed to compete with that? She wasn't unhappy. She loved her job and found it very fulfilling as far as jobs in chemical engineering went, but she was bored. It was time to do something else.

It should come as no surprise that Gen Ys are like this. As social demographer David Chalke says, 'This is the generation that adopted technology as opposed to adapting to it, as Gen Xs did'. I have Gen Y friends who sit watching TV with the laptop on their knee, surfing the net while sending text messages on their mobile phone. Gen Ys were introduced to a multitude of messages and mediums from a very young age. They are excitable, stimulated, technically savvy and impatient. They wait for no man or woman. They grew up in the world of the five-minute abs workout, the two-minute noodle and the one-minute manager, and probably think they're all too slow nowadays.

Internet too slow? Switch to broadband.

Like the sound of that song?
Download the ring tone right now.

Don't like that person? Vote 'em out by SMS.

Don't like that job? Get another one. Online.

'We have got more choice now and that is why you have so many people jumping from one job to another, because we have those opportunities. If you put a choice of drinks in front of someone, they will probably try one of each, whereas if there is only one drink there, they would go for that and be content.'

Contentment is not a principle that is close to the Gen Y heart. Content in their home and family life maybe, but not in the workplace.

Baby Boomers haven't helped this scenario. They've allowed Gen Ys to stay at home much longer than us Gen Xs ever did. The

ABS notes that in 1976, 21 percent of people aged 20–29 were living at home with a parent. By 2001, this had risen to 30 percent. I can remember moving out of home at 21 (after the obligatory backpacking journey around the world) with furniture that didn't match and surviving on pasta for weeks on end. Not this generation. They stay at home much longer, with the double bed, TV, DVD and laptop (on broadband, of course!) in their bedrooms, ruminating over what they might like to do next in life without a second thought as to how it might be funded.

A good friend of mine ruefully points out that it wouldn't matter if he was able to work shorter hours and be home more often to see his Gen Y kids, because they spend all their time in their rooms engrossed in various items of technology, living their own life from what happens to be his postal address, so creating the opportunity for more quality time would be pointless.

This generation was born restless and has grown up loving change. This is as true in their working life as it is in their social life.

'I will want to change. I will probably find something interesting for a while and then want change. There are lots of things I want to do.'

'I want to be an electrician at some stage but I know I want to be a chef before that, so I can see how that would be like.'

'A lot of my mates, we know that we are not going to work in the same job or the same industry for our whole career.'

I will probably have a couple of husbands,
like I will have a couple of different careers

'I will probably have a couple of husbands, like I will have a couple of different careers.'

Spoken like a true Gen Y without any emotional bravado – just the certainty of the future being anything but certain. In the workplace it is no reflection on loyalty, as discussed earlier, but it has enormous implications for the attraction and retention of good staff. And, of course, it speaks volumes about the need for a strong employer brand.

A breathtaking sense of entitlement

Allow me to slap you across the face with a dead fish by sharing two of my favourite quotes with you from the Gen Ys I interviewed:

'What employers need to understand is I'm doing them a favour coming to work. I know who I am, I know what I'm capable of, I know what I'm worth.'

'This might sound arrogant, but I think it's unreasonable to expect that after five years in uni I should have to work for someone else.'

Keep true
to the dreams
of thy youth

Friedrich Von Schiller
1759–1805

Now while we recover from the audacity of these comments, it's worth spending a bit of time exploring where such an attitude of entitlement came from. I lay the blame fairly and squarely with the parents of these Gen Ys.

Why do they have such high standards? What makes them think they should be able to achieve whatever they put their mind to? Why are they so driven by success? Hmm, let's see now. Could it be because we brought them up that way?

I can hear you now – 'What rot, we didn't teach our children to be vain, money-grabbing parasites!' Maybe not. But in an attempt to raise children with strong values of resilience and self-worth, they were told time and again how they were important, valued as individuals, and the sky was the limit for their future. They were entertained in the family holiday house (where previous generations were lucky to get a road trip in a caravan), and they were encouraged not to settle for less, to know their own sense of worth. They were educated to the highest level of any generation in history, creating an expectation that their future would be a shiny and successful one. They were encouraged to question why, and to cultivate their sense of individuality and confidence.

In the workplace, meanwhile, we have stripped organisations down from the multi-layered, hierarchical structures of the past to a more evenly-spread, team-based approach. In an effort to obtain higher levels of performance and productivity, we have relied on the 'one in, all in' concept, where everyone contributes to and shares in the successes, and the failures, from the very start, irrespective of position or length of tenure. One Baby Boomer told me the new graduates in his workplace are actually referred to publicly as 'The Chosen Few'.

Is it any wonder that they are now replaying those attitudes to us? We encouraged them to be individuals, to question the status quo, to have faith in their own convictions, to trust their instincts. And when they do exactly that, we say 'Hang on a minute, who do you think you're talking to?' They want to inherit the earth, because we told them that they

could, but now we want them to hurry up and slow down.

They want to inherit the earth because we told them they could, but now we want them to hurry up and slow down

Gen Y expert Peter Sheahan makes an extremely good point when he says that 'Generation Y have separated effort from reward'. They have never experienced the blood, sweat and tears that go into building a successful outcome the way Boomers and Gen Xs have. They are the fruits of that labour – they have no need to toil themselves.

As a working mother, I have had to come to grips with the feeling of never doing any one job well, of constantly juggling a home life, a work life, a married life and a Penny Burke life. You work yourself into an uncomfortable situation where you feel that nobody gets the best of you.

Just about every other working parent I know feels like that – but not many Gen Ys share this anxiety. Sure, not many of them are juggling the same number of commitments yet, particularly family commitments, but my point is that it's not how many balls they have in the air, it's their attitude towards having numerous balls.

'Of course I want to do well in my career. But the job has to be something that doesn't take up all your time … you want the weekend, flexible hours. So it doesn't take away from your family life.'

So yes, success in the workplace is important, but not if they have to compromise too much to get it. The key difference between Gen Ys and those who went before them is that Gen Y has the law of supply and demand on their side. The skills shortage is such that they can indulge their fear of boredom or stagnation and simply move on to the next greatest thing with no fear of the consequences. They know the score, they have no loyalty, and they know they can get another job easily. And through this, they will force employers to focus.

If we thought their self-expectations were high, their expectations of employers are even higher. Time and again in the course of my research, I encountered conversations indicating that Gen Ys were simply not going to put up with what they perceived to be substandard behaviour by employers. The problem is, some of those behaviours are the modus operandi for many Gen Xs and Boomers!

'I told Maccas right from the start that I wouldn't work the 6am Saturday shift. I would tell them, like, I can't do that because I like sleeping, but the manager just kept on rostering me on so I just quit because he wouldn't listen to me.'

It's worth noting that the job had been clearly advertised as being for the 6am Saturday shift – there was no misrepresentation or unfortunate allocation. That was where the vacancy was, and 'Sleeping Beauty' knew that from the outset. She lasted four weeks before she packed it in. Now we can be outraged by that, but she's already on to her next job, and hasn't given it a moment's thought.

They are a study in conflict, this group – they want it all, they want it laid at their feet and they want it now. They also want Saturdays off and double time on Sundays

The infamous Generation Y ▶

I posed the hypothetical question to a group in Canberra of how they would feel if they had to work in an office building that didn't have air-conditioning. The conversation went like this:

Interviewee: 'You are going to make yourself sick, it would be awful.'

PB: 'Would it be enough to make you go elsewhere though?'

Interviewee: 'I think you would end up going to your Union and saying it was necessary … whoever is in charge needs to be aware that's what employees need.'

This is air-conditioning, people, not access to fresh running water and sanitation. Even for Gen Ys fresh out of university, the expectation is that they will walk into a job with substantial responsibility and an interesting, varied job profile, as opposed to those without qualifications who expect to spend a year or so (but that's all) doing mundane tasks.

'I am not going to do a job without career advancement, and I think a degree kind of proves you are willing to do the work … so instead of starting off with the Year 12 or Year 10 graduates you have already been trained.'

'Hopefully uni will do the job and I will be fully trained before I start.'

I guess there is no need to enrol in the University of Life if you've been to the University of Academia. In a conversation with one Gen Y, I asked how easy she thought it would be to just walk in straight out of university and start calling the shots.

'Easy', she replied. 'Why is that?', I asked. 'I'm just going to do it.'

They expect to advance at work, to be given new challenges, fresh stimulating projects and professional development. They want training, a commitment to life-long learning, and opportunities to prove themselves and extend their skill-set. They're a study in conflict, this group – they want it all, they want it handed to them on a silver platter, and they want it now. They also want Saturdays off, and double time on Sundays if the surf's not running.

This sense of entitlement, not to mention a genuine expectation that their extensive list of conditions will be met, extends not only to the pay packet and conditions of employment, but also to flexibility of hours.

'I think (when) your employer understands that you do have a life outside work and things do happen … I mean you wouldn't want an employer who thinks that you are there for him or her and that's it.'

'I don't ever want to have a full-time job. My perfect job would be 9am to 1pm every week day, or perhaps three days a week.'

'I was being facetious before about the three day week. But hey, if you were in a three-day week and you were providing input, why shouldn't they train you?'

Most Gen Ys are expert negotiators and, as noted earlier, the skills shortage is stacking the odds increasingly in their favour. Needless to say, many of the 40-something employees I interviewed were full of stories about what they saw as outrageously demanding Gen Y behaviour. Equally though, the same 40-somethings are being forced to come to the table. One Canberra-based Boomer told me of his recent journey in hiring a research assistant:

'This woman is saying "I don't want to live in Canberra, at least for the first six months" and I am saying "you've got to be joking" ... Then she is saying "I only want to work three days a week" and I go "well come on, I expect you to work five" ... But it's a buyers market ...'

For the record, he ended up offering three days a week for the first six months, then up to four days a week, with a renegotiation period at the end of the second six months. The realisation is slowly beginning to dawn on corporate Australia that the labour market is changing. We're being forced to focus. As our man in Canberra said:

'We have to change our game, but I still find it a shock. I expect that when I interview someone that they have come for a five-day week. But people nowadays have this thing called a lifestyle – they don't want to work.'

I'm not sure I would agree that Gen Ys don't want to work, but they certainly want a lifestyle, and their expectations are high that their place of employment will play its part in providing that for them. Gen Ys expect the workplace to entertain them as well as train them – they see it as part of the work contract.

'I think it is their responsibility to make it fun. We have to be there a lot of our lives.'

We can lament the way things used to be, and be taken aback by the brashness of Gen Y, but there are as many upsides to a talented, demanding generation as there are downsides. We can't expect to have them highly educated, inspired, driven and passionate and then stomp on them the first time they show signs of demonstrating initiative. Whether or not Boomers and Xs are on board with the concept, they'll find the need to get with the program, because Gen Ys are here to stay, and they have the numbers and the trends on their side.

Why won't they listen?

The final key defining characteristic of Gen Y in the world of work is one that isn't just confined to their group – it is a deeply-held and cherished universal human need that drives their quest for satisfaction – the need to be heard.

When asked what they most want in an employer, they will say 'someone who will listen'. Listening is the number one prerequisite for this group, because it validates their sense of self. It goes arm-in-arm with respect, and you probably won't be surprised to hear that Gen Ys have finely-tuned antennae that can tell them at a distance of 50 paces whether or not they are being treated respectfully.

'I want respect as a person and as a worker.'

'I see it as mutual respect, you have to respect your boss but you need your boss to respect you.'

'I want to have a voice in the company.'

I am not young
enough
to know
everything

Oscar Wilde

'Having a boss who listens and is prepared to listen.'

Listening also relates to positive feedback, most notably praise. Despite all their self-confidence, Gen Ys love to hear that they're doing well.

'To feel appreciated … I have actually worked with (xyz) and the managers are just terrible, they don't acknowledge you or say thank you for your hard work today.'

They want praise, and plenty of it. They are also open to hearing why they are not doing well, providing you can mount a clear, concise argument. Their robust internal sense of self provides them with a thick skin to protect them from criticism, and they generally take advice quite well, if they can see the logic in your views. If the line of argument has holes in it, you're sunk.

Gen Ys are aptly labelled, because of their insatiable appetite for asking the question 'why'? They ask it often, they want a genuine answer, and they want it laid out for them. Gen Ys will not follow rules or procedures for which they can see no logic. They will simply ignore them or, worse, take you on in a deliberate attempt to prove the futility of such constraints.

The solution every time is to explain 'why'. Not only will that improve their learning and development, but it will prove to them that you are willing to listen, spend time with them and help them in their endeavours.

Summary

Clearly, Gen Ys are a challenging and demanding generation to manage, and many Australian companies are starting to understand that already. As I said earlier, I don't believe that a generation's attitudes alone are capable of causing a significant and lasting structural change in a market. However, overlay that attitudinal change with a very real skills shortage and you have the perfect recipe for seismic change.

Gen Ys do appear to have significantly different attitudes to work and work–life balance. While they may still seek security as their parents did before them, their means to that end is quite different. Their sense of loyalty is vastly different to what went before them, and they enjoy a heightened sense of entitlement. They want to be heard. They want to be well paid. They want to have fun. They want to be challenged, stimulated, excited, and rewarded, and they know their true value. And so, it appears, will Australian companies in the very near future.

The infamous Generation Y

04 How do you build an employer brand?

If you've read this far, hopefully I no longer need to convince you of the merit of developing a strong employer brand. You appreciate that a skills shortage is on its way, you understand that the new generation of workers will present particular challenges, so you see the wisdom – however reluctantly – in putting more focus into your internal brand. The question now is how.

Like any brand, your employer brand is about perception – how you want to be perceived by your customers, except that in this case, your customers are your current and potential employees. Research by the Work Foundation and Future Foundation in the US indicates that employees are increasingly behaving like traditional consumers when deciding whether to remain with a particular employer or move on. Isn't that the type of behaviour we should be aiming for? Why would we think it's acceptable for people to have strong brand attachments in relation to material items (such as their Nikes, their Armani or

their Foxtel), yet not feel a similar depth of emotion about where they work? The equipment inside the factory, the fixed assets of the company, will be there forever. However, your people, who hold the intellectual property of the business, can leave at any time. Wouldn't we want them to feel as bonded to their working life as they do to the possessions they accumulate as a result of their work?

The steps one takes to develop an employer brand are actually identical to the steps taken in developing an external brand – but the focus is obviously different. Get the development right though and, just like a robust external brand, it can be used to guide the whole employment experience. Good brands need limitations – remember, it's better to stand for something rather than nothing at all! Once you stand for something, the blueprint of what you can and cannot do becomes clearer, the brand comes into focus, and the tone and manner of engagement is set.

> # Learning without thought is labor lost; thought without learning is perilous
> Confucius 551BC–479BC

Good brands also result in the 'buyers' of the brand becoming evangelists for the brand. This would be a mighty nice place to get to, where your employees and their families and friends become strong advocates for your workplace. We all know the damage a 'rogue' employee, someone who is disengaged and un-empowered, can do, but the benefit of an evangelist is often understated. Greg McKibbin, CEO of Kodak Australasia, spoke of the extremely difficult period when their manufacturing site was shut down and some 600 people lost their jobs. He recalled the media camped outside the front gate of the factory, desperate to find a story about some poor family who were going to be living on the streets as a result of the closure. Greg believed that the fact that they couldn't find one was probably the best example of the power of a strong employer brand, particularly in such difficult and emotionally charged circumstances.

Then there is the question of process. In 2005, I was a member of a four-person team retained to complete a ministerial review into recruitment and retention in the Australian Defence Force. The scope was very large, covering all three services, Army, Air Force, and Navy, both the full-time complement and Reserves. Timelines were short, and crossed the Christmas holiday period. We were a civilian team who, with the exception of one member, knew very little about the ADF, we were part-time, and we were living in different states. It was a daunting assignment, to say the least.

Our team leader, a very talented leadership and human resources consultant by the name of Avril Henry, had stewardship of the project, and did a sterling job of tackling this large, amorphous exercise, putting some structure and context into it, generating a road map for us all to follow, and ensuring we met successive deadlines. Afterwards, I asked her how on earth she had done it. Avril said it was really very simple. Before she had moved into HR, she was a project manager, and it was her project management skills that came to the fore in our project.

A valuable lesson, really. If you expect

wide-scale change to occur, want to develop a direction, need to unite members of a disparate team, begin a journey of learning, and deliver outcomes that are usable … well, projects like that don't just happen. Like any complex, multi-layered task, it needs to be project-managed, with a dedicated team leader, a champion of the cause, and total commitment and buy-in from the top, otherwise it just won't happen.

Having said that, assuming you have your team assembled and you're ready to go, what are the steps involved in building an employer brand?

I call them the five 'A's:

Step One – Analyse

Any good brand must have at its heart the core needs of its target market, the person or people to whom it most wants to appeal. So the first step is all about the target market – your current and potential employees. Who are they, what do you know about them, where will they come from? Who do you most want to reach?

Step Two – Audit

You can't influence an audience you don't know, so the purpose of this step is to develop a very strong understanding of what your potential audience wants. This doesn't mean that you tailor your brand to the whims of what your people say they want, only to change it the following month should they change their minds. The whole concept of marketing involves matching the needs and wants of customers with what the company has to 'sell'. The process is no different for employer branding. It may well be that some people want what you cannot provide. Such is life. The object of the exercise is to make sure that you deliver what the employees you definitely do want working with you truly desire.

Step Three – Aspire

To my mind, this is the most exciting part of the brand development cycle, and the one that's the most fun. It's the part where you get to 'blue sky' a little, to think what might be, to challenge yourselves and your future. In my experience, companies don't do this nearly enough, and so limit their potential. If you don't set a goal, how do you expect to achieve it? I often say in my workshops that if you don't know where you're going, any road can take you there. A little bit of meandering along the road of life is good in a workshop that has been designed with that aim, but it's important to have a purposeful direction so, by the end of this phase, you need to have developed a very clear idea of where you want your employer brand to go.

Step Four – Apply

A psychologist once told me that some people are 'outcome' driven, while others are 'process' driven. Both types of people are pretty important in the development of an effective employer brand, because not only does your company need to develop a clear outcome in terms of where it wants to go, it also needs to develop an accompanying plan to help it get there. As stated earlier, unless there is a really strong implementation plan, there is no way of communicating the new brand focus to the very individuals who desire it the most.

Step Five – Assess

Measure, tweak, monitor, then measure again. Assessing outcomes and holding oneself accountable for achieving objectives is, unfortunately, one of the least celebrated and most poorly executed competencies in companies. I don't know why, maybe it's because measuring is generally considered a lot less sexy than designing, implementing or doing. But it is absolutely imperative, benchmarks and all.

Let's now look at these five steps in more detail.

Why would we think it's acceptable for people to have strong brand attachments in relation to material items (such as their Nikes, their Armani or their Foxtel), yet not feel a similar depth of emotion about where they work?

05

Analyse the situation

Not everyone is equal

Despite the desire of do-gooders for an egalitarian society, the cold, hard reality is: not everyone is equal.

In 1906, Italian economist Vilfredo Pareto observed that 20 percent of Italians received 80 percent of the wealth from the land. This finding was reflected in the work of quality management pioneer Joseph Juran in the 1930s and 40s, who termed what he called 'the vital few and trivial many' the Pareto principle, or the 80/20 rule. Basically, this principle suggests that in any given situation, as a rule of thumb, 80 percent of the results are generated by 20 percent of the causes.

Think about this as it applies to your business: 20 percent of your range of stock might constitute 80 percent of your sales revenue; 80 percent of your stock might come from 20 percent of your suppliers; 80 percent of your sales might come from 20 percent of your customers. Although it is often misused, the 80/20 rule can be applied to many things, including staff.

The underlying value of the Pareto Principle is that it forces us to focus on the 20 percent that matters. Of the list of things you would like to do during your day, the most important 20 percent will deliver 80 percent of the results you want, so it's important to identify and focus on those things.

Not every employee (or potential employee) is going to be a star performer, but that doesn't mean they are not 'good' people, or talented people who are very good at a specific job. However, employment involves the marriage of a number of factors, including skill-set, culture, productivity and performance.

I found the interview with Greg McKibbin, CEO of Kodak Australasia, absolutely fascinating in this regard. Sure, many companies face challenges in the market place, with new markets emerging and older markets maturing, but arguably, not many have faced the challenges that Kodak has in the past five years. 'We have gone through a dramatic change where we have gone from a manufacturing organisation to a sales and marketing group', said Greg. The change had nothing to do with the talents of some individuals, or how good a job they were doing – it was all about the new skill-set that was required. Kodak found they were suddenly playing a totally different game and needed a different type of team on the paddock.

My point is this: you need to segment your audience. You simply cannot expect to attract or retain everyone, no matter how strong your employer brand is, nor should you want to. It's the same as a consumer brand – you have your evangelists, but you also have your switchers, who hop in and out whenever they choose. The trick is to know who is who, and spend the majority of your time and effort (80 percent, perhaps) on the ones that count.

My experience is that people generally do not like compromises (certainly, Gen Ys are not big on them). They may say they like the idea of a compromise … but if it means that everyone only gets part of what they want, is it not better to give 80 percent of people what they want, understand that the other 20

percent are transient, and therefore unlikely to be swayed, and build a brand that stands for something?

So how does a market actually segment if we are talking about employees? For many traditional consumer brands, we generally see a frequency distribution of customers that looks like this:

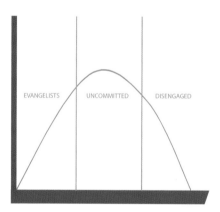

Evangelists are the ones who understand, and are loyal to, the brand without necessarily needing to be directly targeted. A company never has as many Evangelists as they would like. In terms of employer branding, these people are very important, because they are the heart and soul of the employer brand. They are the ones who walk the talk, and they become the cultural epicentre of what the brand is about. You'll know who I'm talking about – there's one in every workplace.

They just seem to embody the spirit of the company; they are the brand. I'm not just talking about high profile CEOs here either – Richard Branson is obviously the key Evangelist of the Virgin brand, but often they are from the ranks of middle management, have substantial tenure, and are popular employees.

Performance studies have also shown that this group generates a disproportionate amount of the success of the business. Success breeds success. Improvements in company performance are often driven by the Evangelists – further evidence of the Pareto Principle at work.

When we talk about the development of an employer brand, however, although the Evangelists are the heart of the brand, they are generally not the core target of the brand. This is because the return on investment is low – you are preaching to the converted. Evangelists are already living the tenets of the employer brand and, although they are always open to further strengthening of

Analyse the situation ▶

employer brand values, and they are the ones who will lead an improvement in external performance, they are less likely to be a core audience for the employer brand process.

They must be intimately involved in the development process, however, because the final brand essence must be consistent with the values and beliefs of this group of people. To develop a brand essence that is in conflict with your most loyal group of employees would spell disaster because they will not recognise, in this evolving brand, the genesis of the company as they know it. They cannot be ignored, because they are the heart and soul of the brand – but they are generally the most engaged, as things currently stand.

At the other end of the scale are the Disengaged. I have discussed in earlier chapters the devastating effect a disengaged workforce can have on productivity and other corporate measures. Although it should be every company's objective to minimise the number of disengaged employees at all times, it is a fact of life that there will always be a small percentage of people in this segment. In fact, one could argue that by successfully developing a brand that has clear and strong boundaries,

you increase the potential for alienation. You can't keep everyone happy all of the time. In brand development terms, this group is not a prime segment for the employer brand either, because they are unlikely to be easily swayed from their opinion base. It would be a bit like political parties aiming their communications at the heartland of the opposing party – it is simply not a good return on investment.

The remaining segment is also the one that is generally the largest, and this is the key target for the employer brand process – the so-called Uncommitteds. The most important feature of this group is that, unlike either of the other two groups, their minds are generally open. Certainly, some will be tending more towards the Evangelist end of the spectrum, and some may be tending more towards the Disengaged, but by and large they are neutral about their place of employment, perhaps engaged only on functional attributes such as salary and basic conditions.

This group is your key target audience for the development of your employer brand. Your quest should be to develop your employer brand to convert as many Uncommitteds as possible to Evangelists. This is an emotional battle! Remember Pareto? Another one of his principles was that human beings are not, for the most part, motivated by logic and reason, but rather by sentiment. So converting an Uncommitted into an Evangelist may not be about giving employees more salary or better working conditions, although for some that may well be all that it takes.

This is where the engagement battle will be fought. Your employer brand needs to move as many employees as possible from feeling neutral towards the company to being positively disposed. This is where you will see the biggest return on investment, the biggest productivity gains, and the biggest difference to the bottom line.

An excellent example of the practical application of this type of thinking was explained to me by Rich Field, Brand General Manager at Virgin Mobile. Virgin Mobile was recently purchased outright by Optus SIMplus, and Rich oversaw the internal marketing effort for the merging of the two companies, which were to be wholly branded Virgin Mobile:

'What you find, the rule of thumb is you're going to get 25 percent of people who are going to embrace it passionately, 50 percent who are going to be indifferent, and 25 percent who aren't going to have a part of it. And the trick is, where do you invest your time and effort?

A lot of time you spend it on the 25 percent who are passionately opposed, but my view is to invest in the 25 percent who are passionately for. You are not going to change the passionately opposed, but the advocates are going to actually make more people passionate.'

In Virgin Mobile's case, they expected 25 percent attrition as a result of the merger, but they haven't even gone close to that. That's a sign of a strong employer brand.

Are the Disengaged a lost cause?

While the Pareto Principle suggests the focus should be on the 20 percent of your workforce from whom you can expect to obtain the best response, which is likely to be the Uncommitteds, this does not mean you should not focus any attention on the Disengaged, for two main reasons. First, because some of the activities you undertake to convert Uncommitteds to Evangelists may also succeed in converting a portion of Disengaged to Uncommitteds. You may never get them to the status of Evangelist, but there will be some that are a little less disengaged than others.

The second and more important reason to consider the Disengaged is that they are also the ones who are most likely to leave the organisation. There are many managers I know who consider the concept of an exit interview as merely a box-ticking exercise that HR requires them

to undertake, rather than as a genuine opportunity for learning. Those who are about to leave a company arguably have no agenda, and so can provide a wealth of information to help shape the employer brand program. There may well be some bitterness for some employees who use the opportunity to fire some parting shots – the key is to sort out the home truths from the ill-founded vitriol.

Further, if what the Gen Ys tell us is true, the concept of long-tenured employees is a thing of the past. I read somewhere of a call centre company that had 100 percent staff turnover every year. Imagine that – losing and training your entire complement of staff every year! The exit interview process would be a full-time job.

But the changeability of the emerging workforce is an opportunity, as well as a challenge, especially as many of them state they are not leaving their position because they don't like the company or the culture – they're just bored. And they get bored pretty easily! It may well be that although the grass always appears greener, when they try the other paddock it may not be as satisfying as they thought.

Rich Field, Brand General Manager at Virgin Mobile, talks about this with great gusto. He has had direct experience with the issue, having previously left Virgin Mobile after three years to go to Coca Cola. Was he unhappy with the job? Didn't like the workplace? Offered more money? No, he was offered the opportunity to launch Coke Zero. Now as opportunities for a marketing person go, that's pretty hard to beat! As Rich said, 'You don't get to launch a new brand of Coke every second day'. Virgin were entirely understanding of Rich's opportunity, and genuinely wished him well. Which improved their chances when they rang him 12 months later to try to entice him back to Virgin Mobile to help integrate the newly merged Optus SIMplus company.

Bruce Mansfield, CEO of Visa, echoes this sentiment: 'I have no hesitation or concerns about people leaving this organisation – they leave with a smile on their face and my best wishes … And I love people saying to me when I see them three or four years later, "Visa was one of the best places I ever worked"'. This is a 'Forced Focus' way of dealing with departing employees.

Adopting such an attitude means that the opportunity to re-recruit is high. A boomerang employee, as they are termed, requires less training, because they already know the people and the systems, and have a shorter lead-time before they start delivering value. Managing the exit process is absolutely critical if a company is to maximise the window of opportunity for re-hiring, but many companies handle exits poorly. Companies need to guard against this type of behaviour, especially with Gen Ys, as not only will they leave and

never return, but you can count on them complaining loud and long about the experience to anyone who will listen – maybe even mounting a blog espousing the shortfalls of their employment experience at that particular company.

So the point is this – even though people leave the company, be they Evangelists, Uncommitted or Disengaged, there is always the opportunity for re-hiring and, generally, this is a good outcome for the employer. The exit procedure needs to be handled sensibly, and the employee celebrated for the contribution they have made, rather than vilified for their decision to leave.

Touching your target

The points we have discussed so far in this chapter are most applicable to existing employees, and the need to know and understand your current workforce, but what of potential employees? One of the biggest potential advantages you have in attracting the right people to your company is your brand – both the external and internal expression of those brand values.

When I asked Greg McKibbin the biggest thing Kodak could offer their employees, he said that it was the opportunity to 'be very proud to work with Kodak because of the brand'. Rich Field from Virgin Mobile said it was the attitude that you're there 'because you really want to work for Virgin'.

Sharyn Schultz at ING Direct said, 'Our

culture is very, very positive, incredibly positive when we compare ourselves with the rest of the banking industry. We have a lot of people who just love working here'. A strong brand has enormous pulling power.

> I can't give you a sure-fire formula for success, but I can give you a formula for failure: try to please everybody all of the time
>
> Herbert Bayard Swope 1882–1958

So how do you find these people? If the skills shortage develops as we suspect it will, the traditional means of attracting personnel may need to be supplanted by a more aggressive approach to finding the best candidates. And you'll need to connect with them early.

Some of the world's best brands have a 'cradle to grave' approach that sees them impacting upon the consumer's consciousness long before they reach

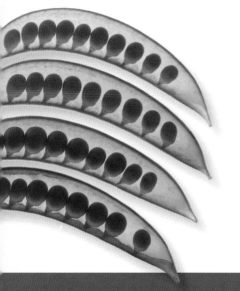

purchasing age. Translated to employer branding, if you know that an eight-year-old boy who is visiting an air show with his parents is likely to make a life-altering decision at that time to become a pilot, where are you in terms of your touch-points with the boys of today who will be your employees of tomorrow?

Having said that, yes, it's true that many Gen Ys will chop and change between various careers and jobs over the course of their working lives. In fact, in the course of my research, I was surprised by the number of Gen Ys who had almost finished the degree course they

candidates should clearly not be treated as one homogenous mass

were currently enrolled in, and yet had already made the decision that their future career would not be in this field. They were no closer to deciding what they were going to do, but they sure as apples knew what they weren't going to be doing! In typical Gen Y style, they were just using the current tertiary course as an interim measure until they either decided what they really wanted to do, or something better came along.

Analyse the situation ▶

Despite their changeability, when it comes to brands, there is no cohort that has ever been as brand-savvy and brand-conscious as Gen Ys. Research at both the University of California and Baylor University medical schools has shown that during the last 50 years, the human brain has 'rewired' itself, and now recognises brand names differently to common nouns or proper names. That's a fairly significant neurological development.

Research conducted by Dr James McNeal at Texas A&M University shows that children as young as 18 months of age are able to recognise corporate labels. At 30 months they associate items and brand names, and between ages two and three they can start to draw brands. By five they are making their own purchases, and by seven they are totally in control.

No parent who has ever experienced a Wiggles concert will question the truth of this finding. My boys are walking, talking Bob the Builder, Thomas the Tank Engine, Dorothy the Dinosaur, Maisy the Mouse, Spiderman, Batman and Buzz Lightyear veterans who are on the endless (and expensive) search for any household or clothing item that bears the moniker of one of their idols.

The youth of today are growing up in a branded world, and brands are all about personality. The workforce of tomorrow is starting to form their attitudes about your brand today, even though they may not be able to dress themselves

just yet. The first time you interacted with a potential future employee, what sort of values did you portray? What impression did you give? Were you warm and inviting, or cold and commercial? What did you stand for? What would the candidate say you stood for?

Generally speaking, perceptions will tend to be much more aligned with the external attributes of what your brand is about, rather than the internal focus of what it means to work at your company but, nonetheless, the attitudes are forming, so best to try to reach them early.

I often use a tool called a Touch Map, which demonstrates the sort of interactions your brand might have with a person over the course of their life. Such a map can sometimes highlight important points in a person's life cycle where the brand could be more visible to them, and so improve the chances of cultivating a candidate for recruitment in the longer term.

Consider the hypothetical Touch Map over the page for a company selling car parts and accessories. This map is a construction that demonstrates a number of valid touch-points for someone engaged in retail marketing of a car parts and accessories brand. It highlights the fact that a person's engagement with a category or brand is fluid over time. I have always found it interesting in marketing terms when I officially entered a new demographic, for example the vord ?　●○　3 yrs. Names car brands　●○　4 yrs. Knows if dad is a Holden or Ford man　●○　5 yrs. Frequent auto retailer visitor　●○　8 yrs. Influences dad on type of car purchased　●○　11 yrs. Loves car computer games　●○　15 yrs. Loves watching motor sport　●○　17 yrs. Saving for car and license　●○

Hypothetical car parts and accessories Touch Map

major age brackets of 18–24, 25–39, 40–54, etc. I somehow suspected that when I woke up on my birthday and found myself in a new demographic, I wouldn't have suddenly adopted a whole new attitude to life. Touch Maps demonstrate that relationships with brands are long term and learned. A person doesn't enter a demographic with a clean slate, ready to be marketed to.

This also applies to employer branding. It may be a long time before a candidate is 'open' for recruitment, but in the meantime, they will have been forming a view of your employer brand for many years.

What are you doing to ensure that those views are positive and reflect the essence of your brand? Sandra Blackburn, an HR practitioner at Pacific Brands, has found that her company invariably has a difficult time recruiting sample machinists and bra designers: 'People aren't interested in the fact that this is a fun place to work, because they would actually rather be working for a smaller organisation like a fashion boutique, and doing something

they see as being more groovy, funky work and design'. The HR task at Pacific Brands has been to re-engineer the job specifications, focusing on university graduates, and to position a job at Pacific Brands as being a good career option in terms of overall experience.

You often hear of employers in small towns or regional areas 'owning the town'. They are the dominant figure in a small country town, with virtually the entire community economically dependent on them. Even in metropolitan areas, you can often see a geographical concentration in terms of 'catchment' by a large employer. That's why Kodak was so concerned about moving its office from Coburg to Collingwood after so many years.

Most employees lived in close proximity to the factory and, in many cases, both partners in a family worked there. It stands to reason that people in your immediate area are the most likely pool of potential employees, particularly when the majority of jobs are not highly skilled, so to relocate would mean losing a large part of your established workforce.

ig buyer
essories.
ervices

21 yrs. Large portion of disposable income on car

28 yrs. Daily driver more functional, has hobby car

35 yrs. Focus on safety and car with kids' seats

40 yrs. Hobby/ dream car. High rates of purchase again

50 yrs. Helps son buy and work on first car

60 yrs. Big spectator of motor sport

70 yrs. Tinkerer in garage

A Touch Map is designed to help you understand that there are numerous occasions when a company has an influence on its current and future employees. Strong brands understand where those touch points are and identify appropriate mechanisms to facilitate brand interaction. Once you've identified the right times to talk to them, the next step is determining what to say.

The right message at the right time

Once a company is in recruitment mode, the pool of candidates diminishes as they work through the process, attrition occurring through choices on the part of both the company and the candidates. This period, which generally lasts anywhere from a couple of weeks to a couple of months, is referred to as the recruitment window.

However, the Touch Map reveals that the real recruitment window, where the employer brand has an opportunity to impact on candidates, extends over a much longer period than that of the formal recruitment process. It highlights the numerous opportunities available to converse with particular targets over a long period of time, all chances to sell the employer brand.

Of course, the company needs to understand the most relevant aspects about which they should be talking to candidates at each step of the journey.

It's no use talking to a young teenager about superannuation benefits when he's still trying to decide if he would like to try engineering or science. Better to inspire him with graphic illustrations of the exciting journey that science can offer, the opportunity for life-long learning, and the camaraderie of the science fraternity (assuming there is some!). When he's reached the stage of comparing the various options at different potential employers, then it may be time to talk in more specific terms.

Talking to potential candidates about what is most relevant to them, particularly during the recruitment process, doesn't sound like brain surgery, does it? But you'd be surprised how many companies treat all the candidates going through the process as a homogenous group. They assume, quite incorrectly, that candidates at the start of the process require the same information as those nearing the end of the process, and that all candidates are identical in their motivation and needs. Good brands find that such a one-size-fits-all approach rarely works well for them.

This was a key finding in our review of recruitment and retention for the Australian Defence Force. The journey for candidates, from an initial consideration of the defence force as a potential employer, through to the point of actually joining the ADF, is a long one. Potential recruits progress through the recruitment

cycle at different rates, and not every recruit moves evenly through every stage, but the basic model looks like this:

The first finding was that candidates should clearly not be treated as a homogenous mass because they have different mindsets at different times in the process. The sort of information you might want when you first consider a role in the Defence Force is different to what you might want when you are about to apply to join up.

A second and more important point in relation to building your employer brand is that candidates access different channels and need to be touched in different ways at each level of the model.

In the application process, for example, the internet is clearly a critical medium for registration of interest, but it is not as relevant at the start of a career choice process because young people are unlikely to surf the net looking for career options.

Part of the process of analysing your target market is making sure you give your brand every chance of engaging with potential employees. A company needs to ask itself a range of questions to this end. Do you know the demographics of your area? The number of schools? The numbers of graduating students, and in what percentiles? Their inclination towards attending university? Their openness to the possibility of scholarships or work experience down the track that could see them positively disposed towards your company? For a long time, work experience has been seen as too hard to administer effectively for many companies. I would suggest that it will become increasingly important to find a way to make it work in the future, because it is a potentially valuable recruitment tool. Have you been to see the schools? Do you have a relationship with them? What is their impression of you, do you think?

If you're finding it hard to orient yourself or your team to thinking about this, try indulging in some 'Forced Focus' thinking. Imagine your industry is in the grip of a paralysing skills shortage. You run ads in Seek, but don't get any responses. The market is so tight that even offering to pay 10 percent more than your competitors yields no results. What can you do? Where will you source your talent from? Think local, think global, think long-term, not short-term. Brainstorm all the options, rank them for efficacy, and then put a plan in place and work towards fulfilling it. This sort of 'Forced Focus' thinking can be relied on to increase your potential recruitment pool so, even if a skills shortage doesn't eventuate, you will have maintained your unfair share of top-quality candidates.

Recruitment advertising versus employer branding

The final point to make in relation to the analysis of your employer brand is to understand that recruitment advertising is not another term for employer branding. Recruitment advertising is just one output of an employer branding process, one of many different outputs a robust branding process will produce. A recruitment ad is a very specific tool, used to hire a person for a particular job.

It's an important aspect of a company's operations, but it is not where the branding exercise starts and stops.

Certainly, you can tell a lot about an employer brand from a recruitment ad. As noted earlier, brand essence reflects the perceived personality of the company, and advertising, even recruitment ads, gives a clear indication of personality. But it is just one of many means to an end for a robust employer brand, not an end in itself.

The entire process of recruitment is a complex, highly-specialised task, and this chapter was not intended to be a rigorous analysis of recruitment procedure. The first step in the 5 'A's of employer branding is about analysing your target and applying some common sense rules of focus to help guide your branding efforts.

A good starting point for the journey of building an engaged workforce is to focus on simple principles, aiming at targets that will provide the best return on investment, rather than at everyone, and ensuring that you deliver the right message to the right people at the right time.

To be conscious that you are
ignorant is a great step to knowledge

Benjamin Disraeli 1804–1881

06

Conduct the audit

At this stage of the process, you will have decided who your target is in terms of the main focus for your brand development. One would assume they will be your current employees, most likely the Uncommitteds. The next step in the development process then is to determine what exactly this group wants out of the employer brand. The second of the 5 'A's in the process of employer brand development therefore is an audit that helps determine what your key target market (as verified by your Evangelists) really wants from you, the employer.

One of the more interesting aspects of the answers that are found in relation to this question is the shift that has occurred over time. In the past, the most usual answer to the question of what employees wanted from their employer was a pretty functional one. They wanted financial rewards, that is, to be paid, preferably rather well-paid. They wanted job stability and, given the economic conditions at various times in the past, it was understandable that this was very important to them. In many countries today, it is still a critical factor. Finally, Baby Boomers and Gen Xs generally wanted good career prospects, and the opportunity to progress up through the ranks.

Although these factors still figure in discussions of what people want in today's work environment, it is fascinating to observe the trend towards the increasing importance of a number

of 'softer' requirements. I touched on some of these earlier with regard to Gen Y, but they are by no means limited to this group. Measures such as a job that will really make a difference, wanting the company you work with to have a high degree of moral fibre, wanting to have a leader who will listen, and wanting to have a voice, are becoming increasingly important. The expectations employees have of their employers are much more fluid – and inevitably lead to a very different style of management, and different requirements of an effective CEO – than those of the past.

Unfortunately, there are some CEOs who haven't noticed this fundamental change as yet, suggesting widespread disengagement at best and outright alienation at worst in many workplaces around the world. Suffice to say, there has been enough written about changes in workplace expectations that the majority of CEOs have at least recognised that the changes are occurring, even if they haven't quite come to grips with the implications for their own organisation, and what they need to do to meet the challenge presented by these new expectations.

In the course of my research, I was able to identify five key factors that summarise what people want from their employers today. I call them the 5 'C's – can you see a pattern emerging here? The 5 'C's of workplace desires are:

- Conditions

- Challenge

- Culture

- Continuous learning

- Charisma

to leave if they can get more money elsewhere (especially those in the 'work makes no difference' category, who are solely motivated by cash), but even Gen Ys display a more rounded view in terms of what they want most from their employer. During my research, I repeatedly heard refrains of …

> Do not hire a man who does your work for money, but him who does it for love of it
>
> Henry David Thoreau

The first 'C' – Conditions

The more functional aspects such as the conditions of employment, which have been highly valued in the past, continue to be important. Aspects such as pay, stability, and the opportunity for progression remain important measures of value and worth. Not many people would happily eschew all of these for the sake of passionate fulfilment (although an evangelist such as anthropologist Dian Fossey, who pioneered ground-breaking research into gorillas, is a good example of such a person).

Yes, money and the security it provides is an important factor, and people are entitled to be paid what they are worth. Gen Ys in particular will be very quick

'You have to work out your priorities in life, like, for example, family and spending time with them and setting up in a job or business whereby you are not spending too much time earning a dollar.'

'A good paid job that I really enjoy doing.'

'I want to be well paid AND I want to make a difference.'

Good CEOs are aware of this, too. Marcus Blackmore, for example, states that 'It is very important that management understands that motivation is not just about money. I don't want to belittle the fact that employees need to be well paid, this is of significant importance. But above all there has to be an absolute recognition that it is the collective

strength of everybody in the company that will ultimately make the difference'.

I was reminded of this recently in one of my own workplaces. I am chairperson of the crèche my young boys attend. This is a community co-operative, with a committee of management comprised of parents of children at the centre. The roles are all voluntary, and can take up substantial amounts of time.

The centre has always enjoyed excellent staff retention levels, far above the industry standard, which is quite low. Child care is a thankless job, involving extremely hard work and very low pay. You wouldn't catch me doing it if it were the last job on earth, yet the people who work in our centre are truly inspiring. They have a calling, indeed they have a gift. They have the patience of saints, and are dedicated, committed individuals. We value them enormously.

Over the last 12 months, we have found it increasingly difficult to attract a top-quality kinder teacher. In one case, after months of searching we decided that we had found the perfect candidate, and she verbally accepted our offer. However, before we could arrange for her to sign the contract, she was offered more money for less hours at a private school kinder, so she reneged on our agreement. It's a tough industry in which to be recruiting good staff.

When the year began, the committee had two main objectives. First, we were involved in extensive planning for an expansion of the centre that the local council was funding. As you can imagine, there was a lot of correspondence to and fro between ourselves and the council, and we were keen to finalise the plans. Second, I had been concerned for some time that we were lagging behind in terms of remuneration for our staff. I was keen to not just look at salary levels, but to review the whole package of benefits for our staff.

Conduct the Audit ▶

We conducted a staff survey, found out what was important to our employees, and designed a package that included a substantial salary increase, better staff-to-children ratios, and more planning time. The committee was pretty proud of the outcome, and we were looking forward to announcing our decision to the staff.

I arrived at the staff meeting full of enthusiasm, and started off by unveiling the architect's plans for the proposed expansion. There was detailed discussion about how the plans would actually work in each room, and then I proceeded to outline the new benefits package. Guess what happened?

Nothing.

There was complete silence. Gone was all the enthusiastic chatter that we had been enjoying just moments earlier. You could have heard a pin drop. As I outlined the improvements in salary and conditions, I was confronted with a room full of Easter Island statues. They couldn't have appeared more disinterested! I made frantic eye-contact with the centre co-ordinator – what was going on?

I ploughed on regardless, limped to the conclusion, muttered platitudes about how much the committee valued them, thanked them for all their effort, and then lapsed into silence.

Eventually, someone spoke.

'Thanks so much for that, Penny. And can I just say, on behalf of all the staff, how great it is to have you share the details of the expansion with us and give us a chance to comment. You could have just proceeded with them without even telling us, and it's just great to get a chance to comment. So thank you.'

Enthusiastic agreement all round.

There you go, then. Sometimes it's about more than just the money! I'm quite sure the staff were very happy about their pay rises, and in the cold light of day the salary is no doubt a key factor in attracting and retaining quality staff. But here was evidence that people increasingly want to be involved in matters affecting their workplace, not treated as outsiders. These more fluid measures of workplace satisfaction are becoming more prevalent, and increasingly being seen by people as part of the conditions of the job.

Many CEOs and companies are now witnessing this trend. The internationally based Walker report found that around half of respondents agreed that a satisfying job in a good working environment was more important to them than salary. Singapore recorded the strongest level of agreement, with 66 percent of respondents saying that job satisfaction was paramount.

The Synovate surveys confirm these findings, and note that factors such as leadership, change management, a stimulating working environment and growth and development opportunities can be just as effective in boosting employee loyalty as salary.

In Australia, a recent survey by the Institute of Chartered Accountants revealed that only four percent of accounting students rated salary as a primary motive for their career choice. And at Virgin Mobile, the marketing director is in no doubt as to why people work at Virgin:

'Virgin doesn't pay the best, we don't … but we are not trying to attract you by paying you lots of money. We want you to come and work for us because you really want to work for Virgin. Because you are passionate about working for Virgin. And if you are not, you are probably not going to last, because it is a destructive environment, it is quite a chaotic environment, and unless you action it and until you believe in what you are doing … you are going to get miserable, and you are going to get miserable a lot of the time about the functional things.'

This indicates specific recognition of first, the power of a strong employer brand, and second, the importance of emotional engagement as a method of building that brand, rather than relying on functional attributes.

Stability, and its relationship with the issue of security, is another interesting factor. Stability may be thought of as staying in the same place for a long time, a notion that most Gen Ys pointedly reject. But security is a core condition that all generations seek, even Gen Ys. Their interpretation of how you get it might be altering, but nonetheless its power remains undiminished. Shane Freeman, Group General Manager of HR at ANZ bank, says that as a result, the HR function has started to see a shift in language: 'I think they have been pretty well trained to feel insecure so functions like mine have been beating a drum for the last ten years about employability rather than security. People say well OK, if I can't rely on employment relationship for security then I won't, and I will become much more mercenary and transactional.'

Stability is still an important factor for employees worldwide. In a recent global survey conducted by Manpower, security and stability was cited as the number one attribute of a great employer by almost half the respondents. However, when you drill down by country and industry sector, a more tailored response begins to emerge. Those in the medical and health care, education, business services and utilities and energy industries were least concerned, as were people in countries such as Belgium, Austria and Denmark. So security remains a factor, but it would seem likely that it will decline considerably in years to come and be less of a concern in certain critical industry categories.

In the course of my research, I found that Gen Y is not terribly concerned about job stability which, to them, invariably carried visions of being stuck in a stable job which would bore them senseless. This doesn't mean that every Gen Y is unconcerned, however. As noted earlier, there are pockets of disadvantage in Australia where stability is a key concern but, by and large, stability is less important than it has been in the past. After all, Australia's unemployment rate is down to 4.9 percent.

In some cases, stability is actually starting to be perceived as a negative. One

research subject in Sydney commented that, 'In fact our HR department would look and say I don't know, they've been with one company for seven years, they might not have flair'.

A number of Baby Boomers felt that Gen Ys did not respect the years of experience they (the Boomers) had accumulated, and felt it was increasingly becoming a constraint rather than an advantage. This reflects the ongoing clash between younger and older generations. This issue was the focus of Ryan Heath's delicately titled book *Please Just Fuck Off: It's Our Turn Now*, published in 2005. The book was a call for Boomers to surrender their influence and stop obstructing more capable Gen Ys in their quest to inherit the earth.

Whether or not you consider the title to be merely an attempt to garner sales-stimulating headlines through controversy, the underlying message was that for Gen Y, stability and tenure is not as highly regarded as change. Boomers and Gen Xs also point to the lack of understanding on behalf of Gen Y of the benefits of experience. As Ronda Jacobs, Managing Director of Cardinal Health, commented, 'I don't think they think experience means anything other than equalling a length of time. And they don't seem to realise that you might actually face a situation and be able to feel more comfortable because you

have faced the same things before. That's what you get with experience, not a longer period of time, and they don't seem to have connected that dot at all'.

This is further complicated when you consider that some employment categories and jobs are in fact genuinely new, and these tend to be the natural domain of the young and the restless.

Again, Kodak provides a good example when Greg McKibbin says that, 'Now, with more digital products, you know we are looking for a different skill-set'. It's not just Kodak who needs them – everyone in that market does. New technology is emerging at an ever-increasing pace. This is not to say that a Boomer couldn't come to grips with new technology any less effectively than a Gen Y. I know some grandfathers who are more obsessive and knowledgeable about technology than I am, but they would likely be in the minority.

So it's clear that the traditional, functional aspects of remuneration such as pay and stability are increasingly weighed up in conjunction with a range of other factors now, and together these criteria are coming to reflect what people want in their work life.

One of the key expectations underpinning conditions is that the employee will be presented with options, and be allowed to exercise choice as to how their conditions will be packaged. Such an expectation of choice is a relatively new notion, as options and flexibility were not exactly the hallmark of employer–employee relations during the era of industrialisation. Now, employees don't just expect acceptable conditions, they also expect some say in how those conditions are delivered.

Take flexibility for example, one of the buzz words of the modern workplace. Many of the CEOs who were interviewed understood inherently the need for more flexible working conditions. Even Boomers recognise that great advances have been made:

'There are a few more things like more part-timers in the workforce now, which never would have happened. A bit more job-sharing, that's a major breakthrough.'

'Flexibility in work hours. Instead of saying you have to be there by 8 am, it is very important to have some flexibility.'

Greg McKibbin recognised the importance of flexibility when Kodak relocated their offices. They had been in the previous location for a very long time, and management went out of their way to accommodate employee groups such as working mothers by offering more flexible working hours.

Again, what is interesting in relation to flexibility is the progression away from the more obvious interpretation of the meaning of flexibility (variable working hours) towards a broader, more holistic definition of flexibility. Sure, non-rigid working hours are the easiest way for organisations to demonstrate their commitment to flexibility, but at the heart of it, flexibility is about a shift in balance towards the preferred terms of the employee, rather than those of the employer.

As noted earlier, flexibility is increasingly being seen in terms of variety of working conditions and choices in the workplace. It is the aspect of choice that is the key here, be it choice of working hours, choice of task, choice of pace, or even choice of boss.

'Say there are different jobs that have to get done, (I would like) the boss to give you the choice of which ones you want to do.'

'I like to take my time in a lot of things I do … I want to be able to put as much time into them as possible, but be flexible enough for emergency situations or if I get sick or anything.'

'I want to be able to manage myself and do what I feel is best – I feel I am good enough at it to know what I'm doing … I want my job to be dictated by myself and what's going on around me so I can respond to it rather than responding to another person.' (From a 22-year-old Gen Y)

'My boss is a distant object. I manage my own errors … I choose my own hours.'

Flexibility as it pertains to variety of work is related to opportunities for development and advancement. Gen Ys in particular see progression as a natural outcome of variety, therefore they see the ability to undertake a range of different tasks as a basic condition of employment. There is an expectation that if you do more and different tasks, you will inevitably advance upwards, even if those tasks are quite unrelated.

'Some sort of advancement program within the actual company so you know you are not going to be stuck doing the same thing forever.'

'I would like my employer to give me the option of increasing my role in my job ... I don't want to do the same thing over and over again.'

And of course, there is flexibility in the sense of work–life balance:

'Understanding of family needs – if I need an afternoon or a day off because one of my kids is sick, I like to get it.'

'They should understand you have a life outside work.'

The key point here is that conditions continue to be an important aspect of what employees want, but their interpretation of what is covered by conditions is becoming much more holistic and a lot less functional now than it was in the past. Employees don't just want favourable work conditions – they want a say in how those conditions will be provided, choice in their approach to working within those conditions and stimulation and empowerment as they go about their work.

The second 'C' – Challenge

One of the more inspiring findings of this research was how thirsty employees were for a challenge. The oft-quoted Gen Y, much-maligned for their apparent flightiness and changeability, were also among the most passionate protagonists encouraging employers to provide challenge and stimulation in the workplace. This was not limited to Gen Y however – many Boomers and Xs were equally driven by the concept of a challenge.

'Setting yourself goals to give you a sense of achievement is very satisfying, because you know you are doing something worthwhile.'

'Challenge in whatever category.'

'Challenges to better myself.'

'If you're not challenged in your work you get a bit stale and you want to be interested in the work that you're doing.'

Doug Shears, CEO of ICM, has a very simple formula for business success which is reflected in the culture of the organisation: 'People Product Profit. Take the first one out and nothing else happens'. This manifests itself in an approach whereby, from the top down, the culture is to give direction, demonstrate the preferred approach, and then let employees have a go, in such a way that the employees are truly able to make the decisions and tackle the challenge in their own way.

As Doug says, 'This has worked extremely well, but you've got to get the right people in place'.

For some people, such an approach means pressure and stress, rather than a stimulating opportunity to enhance their future prospects.

'Realistically speaking, it's a very challenging world today and you have to be on top of everything, otherwise you'll be left behind.'

Some Gen Ys are more than happy to take time off right through to the Christmas break when they finish their tertiary studies, and then begin job hunting in the New Year, but many also feel the oppressive weight of a competitive market for the top jobs, and this brings added stress. They want a challenging job, but they also want to be sure that they will actually get a job at all.

Often inherent in the notion of challenge is the elimination of any likelihood of failure. Failure is not a concept anyone likes to contemplate, and Gen Ys have a greater aversion to it than most.

'I like making a difference. I wouldn't want people saying 'that's great' and I haven't done a thing. So I like knowing that I did it. I want to know that if I want to do it this way, I can do it this way because if I went the wrong way … well … I want a safety net!'

'If I do something wrong he explains why I did it wrong and he doesn't get shitty because it's wasting his time.'

The pitfalls of jobs to which no perceived challenge is attached are obvious, although not many jobs can offer the challenging, exciting nirvana that employees want all of the time. This is particularly difficult for managers of Gen Ys, as numerous parents and CEOs wistfully noted:

'I think it is fundamentally different, because everything is just here and now, and if they are not happy with something they just get out of it.'

'Kids just want to move on – enjoy the experience, enjoy the ride, have fun, then find something different and better.'

'You know it's a stopping off point on the way to something else.'

'The kids want to experience more these days – that's why they find different jobs, different courses, they just want to get out there and fill their life up with lots of stuff.'

'They probably give their best at each thing they do but they don't feel trapped like we felt, they just move on if they are not happy with it.'

A Baby Boomer or Gen X would probably be just as disgruntled if a job wasn't as challenging and stimulating as they'd hoped, but they'd be more likely to stay and stick it out rather than up and leave. As one Boomer confessed:

'I think sometimes you stay in a job because it has been a hard road to hang in there anyway and it is a challenge to stay in a job that is fraught with lack of funding and doesn't pay but given that you get job satisfaction in what you do you tend to stay.'

Spoken like a true Baby Boomer! There wouldn't be many Gen Ys who concur with that line of thought. What a Boomer sees as a challenge, a Gen Y sees as normal, everyday change. Many of the senior managers I interviewed were grappling with what they thought would keep a Gen Y challenged.

Ronda Jacobs at Cardinal Health says one of the unique things in the Vitamin and Supplement industry is the rate of change. Forty percent of their sales are of products that didn't exist three years ago. That's quite an upheaval, one that you would expect would create a sufficiently challenging environment for Gen Y. Ronda talked about one employee who has a degree in biology and started in R&D before moving into marketing, then into business development, and now wants to be a project manager. She is clearly talented, and Ronda is keen to keep her challenged, yet is perplexed by her approach. The employee says she just wants to take the next job that is offered to her, but Ronda wants her to think about whether it's a job she would really like to do, whether she really has an interest in that area. But as Ronda points out, 'She doesn't think like that. She doesn't think what do I want to be – she just thinks what do I want to do – for the next week … the more I talk about what will appeal to these people, the more I feel I don't know what will'.

Amanda Duggan, Group Manager – Customer Marketing at Sensis, relayed a similar story of a graduate who resigned six weeks out from a major multi-million-dollar launch that they had been working towards for a number of months. She didn't have another job to go to – she just felt the time was right to move on. I'm not sure that Amanda felt that way, given that the intellectual property of the project champion was about to walk out the door six weeks prior to the launch.

Given that she was not going to another position, Amanda hoped to be able to tempt her to stay on until the launch in a part-time capacity, with much more freedom and an income stream, but the graduate rejected her offer – not because she was unhappy with the role or organisation, but because she had decided that she had finished her time there, the challenge was over, and it was definitely time to move on.

This seems very curious to Gen Xs and Boomers, for whom the challenge would be consummated with the launch, not six weeks prior to it. When I described this event to a Baby Boomer ex-CEO, he light-heartedly said that if it had happened in his company 'I would be waiting for her in the car park with a baseball bat. What about team? Doesn't team count for anything, the fact that everyone else has now got to run around like lunatics?' This incident speaks to a very different interpretation between generations as to the meaning of a challenge.

Paul Thompson from SCA sees a difficult time ahead in terms of the relationship between the notions of challenge and stability: 'I think there are definitely a lot of people who come out of uni who are really bright, really intelligent and really great pickups … but I think it is harder to find good people who will stay, who will accept the challenge for long enough to add value in the role … You can't learn about a market, put a plan in place and know that it is successful unless you stay around to see if it is successful and know you are truly learning things'.

So the second 'C' in terms of what employees want – challenge – is both an exciting opportunity and a giant management headache for the employers of today. Employers need to work hard to design every position so that there are challenging elements, irrespective of the inanity of the actual job itself. The best way to build challenges into any job specification is through the intelligent use of goal-setting.

The charge towards providing greater challenge in today's workplace is most likely to be led by Gen Ys, but the things that make Gen Ys a most exciting generation to work with also make them the most difficult to manage.

'I think the kids nowadays have better vision, a bigger, broader vision than we had back in those days.'

'They are great – they are fresh, they are new, they are eager, I think it is great, I love young people coming into our workplace, I love training them.'

The difficulty for the employer is to harness the vision, the freshness and the enthusiasm, and then present that back to employees as part of the employer brand. Clearly, the brand alone cannot entirely overcome the realities of a job that might be mundane and boring, but the creation of a stronger employer brand that mirrors the attitudinal tenets that identify Gen Ys in particular will go a long way towards making their workplace a more attractive option.

The third 'C' – Culture

When we looked at the question of what Gen Ys want at work earlier, the issue of culture was seen to be paramount. In short, culture is basically the normative behaviour of the organisation – 'the way we do things around here'. Of all the 'softer' aspects of emotional engagement, culture is the one that is most likely to tip the balance either for or against a potential employer.

The Hays survey found that people judge a company's potential as an employer primarily on their fit with the company's vision, culture and values, followed by the product or service they deliver, and any experiences the person has had as a customer of the company. More than 60 percent indicated that they would not apply for a job with a company whose culture they didn't identify with. A further 23 percent said they would resign if the company wasn't seen to live up to the culture it promised.

This is where 'Forced Focus' becomes important, because some companies are so intent on their external goals that they pay no attention to maintaining a strong internal brand. While this may have been acceptable in the past, it's certainly not going to sustain those companies in the future.

Incidentally, I've always found the term 'human resources', and now the recently trendy term 'human capital', a little disconcerting. They're not really the warmest of phrases, are they? They make you feel as though you, the intelligent heart and soul of the organisation, are

One of the reasons Virgin's management was so keen to entice Rich Field back from his excellent adventure at Coca Cola was because of his previous work as a 'cultural advocate'. Heading into a merger, maintenance of culture was going to be more vital than ever: 'Some parts had Optus culture, some Virgin … how do we manage that? How do we hang on to the stuff which is really important and not die on the sword with the stuff that isn't? So that's a big part of my role – trying to get that right, ensure that the culture is translated, ensure that the brand stays alive and strong'.

And for Gen Ys, a whopping big chunk of that is about having fun, and enjoying the connection with their workmates.

'A good working environment in that you are sort of like around people who are sort of similar.'

'I mean, the hours you've got to be there, you don't want to work with people who you really don't like and don't get along with.'

'Personally, it should be fun.'

'Where I work is really lonely, so where I go I don't really care, I just want to have a social job and somewhere I am going to be happy.'

'A friendly environment, good working relationships.'

'More of a team atmosphere in comparison to a rigid hierarchy as such.'

right up there with the computer network, the car park and the photocopier. So when employees say that the thing they want most from their employer is the opportunity to make a difference, to be treated as an individual, to be listened to … well, it seems a little contrary to refer to them as resources, or capital.

Be that as it may, a culture that encourages a sense of empowerment is clearly critical. Bruce Mansfield at Visa says he believes most organisations would be going through some sort of process focusing on their culture, 'and it's certainly something that I have placed more importance on over the last couple of years'. Virgin Mobile is another company that, not surprisingly, focuses on culture as a key organisational imperative.

Again, Virgin understands this extremely well, and a key component of their employer brand is fun. 'Ultimately it's all about having a lot of fun while we do all the work stuff', says Rich. And with Virgin, you get the impression that they probably do. In fact, one of the more interesting aspects of Virgin Mobile (and, I'd suggest, any company in the Virgin group) is the marriage between the external and internal brands. They invariably appear to be almost identical.

Get the alignment right between your internal and external brand identity and you have a much easier row to hoe. ING Direct is aware of this, with Sharyn Schultz noting how important an effective culture is in building a high performance work place: 'I don't know whether functionally we do anything different, I think it's the way we do it that is different, which gets back to the fact that choosing the type of people to fit into this environment is incredibly important. If you don't fit the culture it's not going to work, it's just not worth it'.

Interestingly, this is not just about seeking a fun, happy way to pass the hours – there is widespread recognition that good working relationships make the job easier for everyone, and produce better results. The notion of teamwork is inherently built into Gen Ys:

'A working environment where people feel comfortable with each other and know what their position is and what they are actually meant to be doing, and realise how if they don't get something done it affects the next person in their job.'

The importance of this sense of teamwork is something that employers are now recognising. When Virgin Mobile are hiring new employees, potential recruits are required to meet the basic set of skills the position requires, but to ensure cultural fit, they then progress through two or three rounds of 'essentially culturally formative interviews … are they going to fit with the culture, are they going to be able to work within our environment, are they going to work with us? There's a huge cultural element there', says Rich.

For Virgin, it is a relatively formal process. The corollary is seen in the approach of a company such as Kennards Hire. Andy Kennard had been the main owner of the business since 1991. Kennards bought a business and with it came some personnel, one of whom would turn out to be the next Managing Director of Kennards, Peter Lancken. At that time, Kennards had (and still have) very little in the way of formal cultural guidelines, and had resisted the HR trend of the eighties and nineties to draw up a list of warm and fuzzy values and print them on coffee cups. However, their culture and values, particularly at a senior level, were, and still are, extremely strong. This is particularly interesting given that Kennards is a family-owned and operated business. Often, such businesses are unable to promulgate

their culture when the founder or owner, who has invariably built the business in their own image, moves on.

One sometimes wonders about Virgin's ability to maintain a strong vibrant brand both internally and externally, beyond Branson. It is a tribute to both Andy and Peter that they see culture as such a central part of their internal employer brand, and together they have worked hard to maintain a very strong sense of that brand over the years. Peter remembers the subject of culture being raised in his very first job interview with Andy. The focus of their conversation was not the financial future of the business, nor what Peter's skill-set could bring to the table, but rather, how Peter proposed to manage the cultural transition from Andy to himself and how he proposed to maintain the (unwritten) cultural spirit of the business.

As the above example suggests, culture is often reflected more in the unwritten rules of the organisation than in the written ones. This is an important aspect for Gen Ys, because they are very quick to rail against rules, especially ones they see to be outmoded, and this directly affects their assessment of the culture. One Baby Boomer was telling me about her Gen Y daughter's brief stint in a law firm, where she wasn't allowed to have hot food for lunch, because it was decreed that the smell would waft through the office and possibly upset clients. Employees

Honesty is the best image

Tom Wilson
Ziggy (Comedian)

were only allowed to bring sandwiches for lunch, and were also required to ask for permission to go to the bathroom. You can imagine how long she lasted.

Now whether we consider this approach outdated, or entirely the prerogative of the employer, the fact remains that such conventions are very clear indicators of the culture that exists within an organisation. They need not be written down, nor included in any employee contract, but they become a far more meaningful indicator of the accepted code of behaviour than anything that is formally documented. Employees can interpret the prevailing culture in the blink of an eye, so employers need to be aware of the signals they are sending with their workplace conventions.

It has long been recognised that a more constructive cultural environment is one that focuses on achieving desired results.

This is particularly important for Gen Ys, but it's no secret that all human beings respond favourably to praise, and it can be a highly-effective motivational tool. As Paul Thompson commented, 'If you say someone has done something bad you only have to tell them once, if you say they have done something good, you have to tell them three times. Frequency is important'.

The February 2000 issue of the Academy of Management Executive quoted Professors DeNisi and Kluger, who

Conduct the Audit ▶

commented that, 'The positive effect of feedback on performance has become one of the most widely accepted principles in psychology'. A workplace that genuinely recognises and celebrates the contributions of its employees often has an extremely strong and attractive culture. The issue of praise and recognition brings me to the final, and probably most important, point about culture, and one of the most critical aspects that should be reflected to employees …

Respect.

As Peter Sheahan says so often, 'Control is out, respect is in'.

Gen Ys often refer to the presence or otherwise of respect as being a key determinant of the culture, and therefore of their satisfaction at work. I believe that this new-found desire for respect is one of the more obvious signs that Baby Boomers have successfully managed to raise a generation of resilient children. These young people have finely-tuned bullshit meters, and they simply cannot be duped. One Gen Y told me of his experience at one of the Big Four accounting firms:

'They sort of talk to you to reward you, they just tell you and think that's enough … they trick you into thinking you are doing really well and moving really high up but you are going nowhere.'

They know real respect when they see it, hear it and feel it. This is not something you can manufacture, not something you can fake – it has to be from the top down, and it has to be the real deal.

'They should respect you and you should respect them.'

Marcus Blackmore notes that this has manifested itself in his organisation as an unwillingness to ever sack an employee. He recalls that he once sacked three people in one day, and for many years afterwards, the staff referred to it as Black Friday. He learnt that, 'You don't need to sack people, you just sit down with them and say we've obviously got a problem, you don't need to go home unhappy at night, nor do I. More often than not, when you approach it in that way, they'll go home and think about it, and then come back the next day and resign. And that preserves their dignity. I think it is important that we try and preserve people's dignity and respect them as individuals'.

This approach has also seen the demise of the policy of an initial three-month probation period for new employees. As Marcus explained, 'We bring a new person in, we say these are our values and they are these non-measurable things like trust, integrity, honesty … and then we turn around and say by the way, we are now going to put you on probation for three months because we don't trust you. I don't think you can do that! You have to look after people and live what you say'.

The absolute bottom line, not only for

Gen Ys but for all employees, in terms of respect is honesty. The days of the corporate cover-up are gone. You can look employees in the eye and say yes, yes, yes – but your actions will speak louder than words, and tell them that you're intent is really no, no, no. The underlying essence of respect is truth, and there can be no false roof in this brand house.

The fourth 'C' – Continuous learning

Young people in particular believe that they possess a unique set of talents that are just waiting to be recognised by their employer. But they don't just want their skills recognised. In line with their preferred culture discussed earlier, they want those skills nurtured and grown during their time with the company. More and more CEOs understand that the employee's time at the company is focused on improving their resumé, and as soon as this improvement ceases, they will leave. Therefore, the opportunity for continuous learning is a key retention device, especially for Gen Ys.

The concept of continuous learning has enormous currency with the ambitious segments of Gen Y, because it speaks to their insatiable appetite for self-improvement.

'Definitely yes (to training), you need the credentials really to move anywhere.'

'You want to get more and more knowledgeable and even if you don't progress in terms of pay, you progress in terms of your knowledge and your experience and doing it better.'

'They have a successful graduate program and they have an internal regime of moving people around into different areas to get different experiences so that would be one good point.'

'The fact that you are learning.'

The global Manpower survey found that, aside from salary and bonus packaging, employer-sponsored training courses and education were cited by 62 percent of respondents as the most valued employer benefit. Educational institutions will become more and more important features on the future labour market landscape. Interestingly, it is not only continuous learning to take you higher in your current role that is valued. Gen Ys in particular are as happy to ride the snakes as they are to ride the ladders, so long as it leads to an overall improvement in their skill-set and an improved level of employability. Of course, this comes with one proviso – learning is good, but skilling is better:

'I have noticed the word multi-skilling is pretty well entrenched into the workforce now.'

'Not being pigeonholed into one job – recognising a broad range of skills and giving you the opportunity of developing them.'

The opportunity to engage in continuous learning is one of the more functional aspects of the employer offer that feeds employees' engagement with a brand. But Paul Thompson at SCA sees the future of training heading into more emotional areas:

'I genuinely don't think that what we call training today will be recognised as training. I think there is an evolution where people are saying training isn't necessarily shipping you off to Harvard University. Baby Boomers would say that is training. Training is now more about experience, and I think employers will talk more about giving you the experience of doing this as an investment in you'.

Gordon Howlett, CEO of Thorn Australia and New Zealand, agrees and believes some work-based training has begun heading in the wrong direction: 'A lot of training forgets the basics. If you know the basics you have competence, and if you have competence you have confidence. There is no point giving six week training on putting people first, and culture, and understanding my role in society, if a customer comes up to you and says I want a fridge, and your employee can't help her because she doesn't know enough about the fridge. I think there needs to be a reinvestment in basic training, again and again and again before you get into the soft skills'.

The development of the entire employment experience reflects the creation of the employer brand, in the quest for greater employee engagement. Companies will be forced to focus on whether or not they are a true learning company, and can offer continuous learning to a future workforce hungry for anything they can provide.

The fifth 'C' – Charisma

The fifth and final element of what people want in their workplace is Charisma, and all that is embodied in the notion of leadership. There are entire books written on leadership and I don't pretend to cover the topic in detail. However, the research indicates some consistent themes in relation to what employees are looking for from leaders, and these themes are worth exploring.

Firstly, it was heartening to see a meeting of the minds between employers and employees regarding the importance of leadership in the workplace:

'I think leadership and morale, certainly leadership, is something that is underestimated as to how important it is.' (Kodak)

'I believe they are still looking for more and more leadership … leaders who have an appreciation of what it really means to be a good leader rather than (a) good manager.' (Visa)

'Leadership is something that hasn't really changed actually. I think good managers always displayed great leadership, it was important then and it's important now.' (Kennards)

'I like to define it as individuals having the courage and the confidence and the passion to engage in this environment and enable others to be the best they can be.' (Peter Sinclair, SCA)

'Leadership is actually about identifying the future. A leader is a person who identifies and shows people that the future is possible.' (The Body Shop)

'Companies that are successful have leaders who are connected with the total organisation, no matter what level it is.' (ICM)

'I think there is a big imposition on the leadership of an organisation to demonstrate values – most people are followers in life, they are not leaders … so it is incumbent on them to truly lead the workplace.' (Blackmores)

It was clear that many workplaces are still grappling with exactly how to demonstrate leadership, especially when they realise that they may not have the necessary leadership skill-set. However, the issue of charisma and leadership is yet another area where 'Forced Focus' will result, because the workforce of the future has pretty high expectations.

'I don't need someone sitting looking over my shoulder the whole day reviewing every time I have a bit of a stretch or whatever, but I want a workplace. If I wanted a social environment, I would be a waitress. I want a serious workplace and I expect professionalism during the hours that we are working, I really insist on that.'

'You want to feel like you are doing something you enjoy doing, and I think the bosses have a lot to do with that. Because if they make you feel you are not doing a good job, you are going to think you are not doing a good job.'

Leadership is not just about setting the parameters – that's the easy part. Employees are actually looking for more than just talking the talk – they want their leaders to genuinely engage with them on their level, to set the example, to interact with dialogue rather than delivering a monologue, and to motivate them and be responsive to their needs.

'If you think something is wrong you can always tell them and if you think they are expecting too much you can tell them you can't handle it, or if they are not appreciating your work you can bring it up with them.'

'If they take an active involvement in how you do, you know, walk into your office every now and then and ask you is the temperature OK, how are you feeling?'

'A really positive level of interaction … a sense of humour.'

This is a minimum performance requirement as far as Gen Ys are concerned. If you're a CEO who expects to be treated in the 'manner to which I have become accustomed', then you had better 'un-accustom' yourself pretty quickly if you hope to engage your workforce in the future. A lot of effective leadership is not about what you do, but about how you do it, which is very interesting, given that the same applies to building a strong employer brand. Above all else, employees are looking for positive empowerment.

'Understandably if there is someone in an authoritative role above you they have to whip you into line if you are doing something wrong and be assertive, but there are ways of doing that, bringing the most out of the people below you.'

'To make you feel like you are all working towards something rather than working for your own goals.'

The 'how you do it' is counter-intuitive for many CEOs. As Gordon Howlett notes, good leadership means, 'Employees have to believe that you are capable of doing it, but you also have to be capable of allowing them to do it. So there is really this transfusion of your skills across to them and giving them the self-belief that they can carry that banner'.

The preceding discussion on what motivates both Gen Ys and the wider workforce provides the best advice to companies wanting to improve their charisma and leadership. A strong employer brand will reflect the notions of a workplace where leaders truly listen, empower individuals, reward their efforts and challenge them to improve themselves.

Summary

The 5 'C's of Conditions, Challenge, Culture, Continuous learning and Charisma provide valuable insights for the Audit step of the brand development process. You can't influence what you don't know, so the first step in the development of an employer brand is to understand what your people want, both functionally and emotionally. Senior management are beginning to understand that a combination of these aspects will be required to meet their employees' expectations. As Ronda Jacobs notes, 'I think that today we are supposed to provide this whole experience – flexibility, different work environment, home, travel, office … and a high degree of change. Whereas years ago we probably were the opposite – we wanted it all to stay the same so we could stay in the same company for 20 years and feel comfortable'.

This 'total experience' factor has also had an effect on the company benchmarking process. Traditionally, Cardinal Health had benchmarked their performance against their direct competitors within the same industry, but once they learned who their employees thought their competitors were, their focus broadened significantly. The people who worked on the factory floor didn't just see their competitors as other pharmaceutical companies – far from it! They saw all other manufacturers as competitors, and the thing they liked most about the Cardinal factory was that it was very clean, and not very noisy in comparison to the factories of other businesses that they saw as being in their competitive set.

Graeme Wise noted the same at the Adidem group (The Body Shop is one of their brands). He noted that many of the ladies who worked in his group's factory chose to work there because it was close to where they lived. Their choices were largely influenced by geography.

The point of this chapter is to encourage you to think about your offer from your employees' perspective, not just on the basis of what you think you want the company to be. Yes, this is hard. The workforce of the future looks like a looming headache for everyone, particularly CEOs and managers. But the future will hold what the future will hold, and 'Forced Focus' is about navigating through the turbulence in order to find clear airspace.

At the end of one long research session I conducted with a group of Gen Ys, we discussed their underlying constant thirst for more, better, higher, faster, more highly paid. I asked them why they expected more. After a short pause, one of them said quite simply,

'Because we are given more.'

Conduct the Audit ▶

This is the conundrum that is our future workforce, and the challenge that will be required to manage them. The more challenges we give them, the more they want. The more we recognise their achievements, the more praise they will crave. The more we reward them, the more they will want. The more training we give them, the more they will expect.

It will require a 'Forced Focus' in workplaces, with the risk of uncertainty balanced against the risk of consequences of failing to adapt. There is the risk of investing in them, knowing that they might leave, the risk of training them and in so doing making them more attractive to a competitor, the risk of making the workplace so much fun that they won't do any work.

This all needs to be balanced against the risk of not investing in your people, and therefore having a habitually disengaged workforce, the risk of not training your people, rendering them incapable of competing with your competitors, and the risk of boring them to death by failing to stimulate them.

There is no simple solution, but it comes back to one thing: engagement.

A successful employer brand is about finding out what its people want, and then proceeding to address their needs in a genuine, committed way, to the best of their ability. When a company does that, risk becomes opportunity.

One person with
a belief is equal to a force of
99 who only have interests

John Stuart Mill 1806–1873

Confirm your aspirations

The first and second steps of the development of an employer brand have now been undertaken. You have done your Analysis to determine who your key target is, and you have completed an Audit so you know what they want. The next step is, to my way of thinking, the most exciting – clarifying that to which you Aspire.

It is often said that if you don't know where you're going, any road will take you there. A large part of 'Forced Focus' thinking is setting your aspirations high, and then working backwards from there. It is much easier and more effective to set out the path after you have determined your end goal, rather than meander along in some general direction, and be happy with some vague iteration of what you imagined eventual success might look like.

Another important aspect of 'Forced Focus' thinking is that it makes you and your management team disciples to both the process and outcome. The heart of what you aspire to, the core of your employer brand, is your brand essence. Your management team must agree upon what that is, be prepared to demonstrate it in words and actions, and live up to it. The employer brand essence will determine the culture of the company, and foster the code of behaviour for both employer and employees.

This chapter explains a number of tools that you can use to help you design your brand and, in particular, its essence. As I have said before, the process is exactly the same as that used in developing an external brand, but with a few justifiable nuances. All the tools are geared towards the pursuit of a strong brand essence, the heart of the employer brand. Before we explore these, first we will look at a few of the features of a good employer brand essence:

A proposition

Once upon a time, when products on shelves were actually different from each other, the marketing catchcry was all about the USP – the Unique Selling Proposition. Large amounts of research were done to uncover the most unique aspect of the product or service, and this became the brand essence upon which the product was marketed. USPs

Change your thoughts
and change your world

Norman Vincent Pearle 1898–1993

definitely had their time – although one could argue that time is now largely over because, generally, products no longer contain any truly unique attributes. The speed to market is such now that if a truly unique product appears, a copy will be on the market inside 12 months, eliminating the claim of uniqueness.

The employer branding equivalent of the USP is referred to by some as the EVP – the Employee Value Proposition. That

Confirm your aspirations ▶

is, the proposition you put to a potential employee that best sums up the offer you can make. Whether you call it an EVP, a brand essence, or the core truth, it is basically the same thing. Employees need to understand what you are about when you talk to them about your brand.

Now that sounds simple doesn't it? But as we will discover as we proceed, sometimes it's not quite as easy as it looks! There are several reasons for that, not the least of which is an unwillingness on the part of employers to commit to any one particular direction.

Better, it is often felt, to just put forth a list of things we do well, and let people sort it out for themselves, which is rather like throwing a whole lot of spaghetti at a wall and seeing if any sticks.

Sometimes, we genuinely don't know. We might feel like we don't have anything unique to offer, and we don't really know why people choose to work here rather than somewhere else. If that's the case, then you need to go back and do step two, the Audit, again. You have to know what people want before you can meet (and exceed) their expectations.

Sometimes the proposition is not actually a proposition at all. There are some consultants who like to deliver warm, fuzzy slogans that they believe sum up a brand essence, but I'm not one of them. They'll say an essence is 'People who really care', or 'A workplace that suits your life', or 'Because we can.' I'm sorry, but I don't consider those to be brand essences, or even propositions, for that matter. What on earth do they really mean? How does one interpret what exactly the company is all about from such statements? What does that say about the employer offer? People don't need sexy statements; they need to be able to understand what the company essence is – they need to know what the brand is all about.

Sometimes the proposition might be accurate but difficult to explain to your employees, as Graeme Wise discovered with The Body Shop. For years, their mission statement focused on being the best retailer in Australasia. As Graeme said, 'Following that through, the accountants were not to think of themselves as wonderful accountants – they were to think of themselves as being wonderful retail accountants, so we made sure the retail business sung', and so on throughout the organisation. As Graeme admits, he struggled to sell this proposition: 'I had real trouble. I had trainers saying if I am the best trainer, that's the only thing I really want'. The point Graeme was trying to make was that you can be the best trainer you want, but unless it adds to the organisation's ability to be the best retailer, then it is a moot point whether it is worthwhile. Some might see this as an exercise in semantics, but it was a very real sticking point for the organisation.

So what did they do? They changed their mission statement! The organisation now has 'the three circles of responsibility' as its mission. One circle is economic success, another is stakeholder performance, and the third is positive social and environmental change. 'Every decision we make in the organisation we examine in light of these three circles. Is it economically viable, is it going to make our stakeholders fulfilled whether they be customers, staff, externals, government … and the third thing, is it going to contribute positively to social change or is it going to have a negative effect. And if it violates any of those three things we will say let's think of another way of doing it', says Graeme.

I think this is a much better expression of The Body Shop's employer brand, because it picks up the social consciousness aspect, something that has been a strong part of the brand's international identity. And of course, this social responsibility aspect is something that we know is highly appealing to Gen Ys in particular. To me, the three circles of responsibility reflect the true personality of The Body Shop, as well as helping to define the spheres of influence for the business.

What is of even greater interest though is the fact that Graeme orchestrated the change because he recognised that as a proposition, the previous statement didn't resonate with his people. 'It is still complex, but it is much easier to explain to people', he says, and that's got to be a good thing.

Something Different

Good brands stand for something in the minds of their customers, something that sets them apart from other brands. Volvo means safety, Kleenex means softness, Coke means refreshment. Generally speaking, two brands can't mean the same thing and, as was noted earlier, it is better to stand for something than for nothing at all.

Your employer brand essence should at least be differentiated from that of your direct competitors, and preferably also from as many other companies as possible. Your brand essence should clearly convey a message outlining the sorts of activities your company could get involved in but, more importantly, it should identify the areas that are inappropriate in relation to the company brand.

Medtronic is a fascinating example of this principle. Medtronic is a US-based biomedical engineering company, best known for their earliest invention – the implantable pacemaker. Their history of innovation and commitment to the progress of human welfare has been a mainstay of their brand essence over the years. The founder of the company wrote the company mission in the early 60s, and not one word has changed since then, yet it continues to differentiate them and provide a beacon to guide everyone forward. One of the key planks of their mission is recognition of the personal worth of employees, a commitment they take extremely seriously, with the end result that Medtronic has achieved Fortune 100 Best Employer status in the United States for eight of the last nine years.

Relevance

Some brands, in an effort to be different and unique, end up with something that is certainly different, and often unique, but not necessarily relevant. It may be true that one of your major points of difference is your length of tenure, but is that fact relevant to prospective employees? Greg McKibbin told me that when Kodak closed down their manufacturing site, the average age of the workforce was in the mid to high forties, and the average tenure was more than twenty years.

This is an awesome statistic and an amazing achievement, something to be celebrated, but it was a sign of times that are rapidly disappearing. Should it be the focus of the future employer brand?

Simplicity

The thing about marketing and branding is that, despite the relative importance we place on it, in the greater scheme of things, it's really not that mission-critical. It's not a cure for cancer, nor is it a solution to world famine, and it doesn't begin to address the complexities of global warming. People are simply not interested in wading through large amounts of paper to find out what your company has to offer. Gen Ys in particular will abandon ship, rather than spend an inordinate amount of time reading the instructions. A good brand essence must be simple.

Authenticity

In addition to containing a clear proposition, a good brand essence must also ring true to employees. A 22-year-old Gen Y in Adelaide told me that he would never work for a company like Exxon Mobil, despite them being the biggest in the world and purporting to be the best, and whose web site states that 'Exxon Mobil Corporation is committed to being the world's premier petroleum and petrochemical company'. 'They were the last to acknowledge global warming. I wouldn't want to work for someone like that'.

His issue was not so much about the scope of work, or the size of the prize, in terms of the pay packet or career progression. He couldn't believe that the world's premier petroleum and petrochemical company would not acknowledge global warming. Done deal. Not a brand for him.

The Brand Pyramid

There are two main tools I use to determine a brand essence, and I will explain both of these in detail. The first is the brand pyramid, which is a well known tool in marketing circles. In terms of its structure, variations of this tool have been presented in pretty much every shape imaginable. Apart from a pyramid, I've seen the staircase, the temple, the football, the onion, the circle, the funnel, the cone and the square, and I'm sure there are others out there!

These tools are generally similar, and the key is that they are 'Forced Focus' tools. Often it is not so much the actual words used, or the ways in which groups of words are arranged as the progress of a group of senior managers through a process, whereby they buy into a brand essence together, and then commit to living that essence. That is the important aspect, and there will be more on that in the next chapter, where we Apply what we have created.

A brand pyramid looks like this:

PERSONALITY

VALUES OF EMPLOYEES

EMOTIONAL REWARDS

FUNCTIONAL BENEFITS

ATTRIBUTES

BRAND ESSENCE

There are a couple of tricks to keep in mind when building a good brand pyramid, but the most important point is to keep in mind how it will assist the process of 'Forced Focus'. By this I mean that rather than including every aspect of your brand in the pyramid, you force yourself to focus by allowing only the three most important elements to appear in each level of the pyramid. The only part of the pyramid where we allow more than three words is in the Attributes section – if you happen to have a brand that is rich in attributes, more power to you.

The debate that takes place among your management team in order to agree the three most relevant aspects at each level is the first and most valuable step in determining your Aspiration.

The second trick is to construct the brand pyramid in terms of the desired outcome for your brand, not the current situation. This is the whole point of the Aspire stage – shining your light into the future, determining the best outcome you can envisage, and then working back from there.

The third trick relates to the people who participate in a brand pyramid-building session. When I run these workshops, I try to get every key stakeholder together in the room at the same time. Australians talk of their preference for 'people to be inside the tent pissing out, rather than outside the tent pissing in'. This quaint colloquialism is about ownership. If you give your key people a chance to get involved and have their comments heard, they will be more likely to take ownership of the outcome. If you leave them on the outer, you give them a reason not to engage in the process, let alone adopt the outcome and, in some cases, an opportunity to actively agitate against it. While we try to keep workshops to a manageable level, I would always err on the side of involving people and dealing with larger numbers, rather than excluding them and then trying to cope with the inevitable consequences.

The final trick is a further example of 'Forced Focus' thinking, and involves the application of strict time constraints for the completion of your pyramid. It is simply unproductive to have your senior management team tied up for lengthy periods navel-gazing about minutiae of expression. If the debate is focused on whether or not the company can be true to a particular essence, then that is a good use of time. If the team is bogged down arguing the case for 'competent' as opposed to 'capable' in a statement of desired personality,

Confirm your aspirations

then they have clearly lost their way. Set yourself a maximum of half a day, get some 'Forced Focus' happening and start building that pyramid!

So what is each level of the brand pyramid about, and how do you fill it out?

Attributes

The attributes of your brand are the tangible aspects of your brand that you can see or touch. They do not have meaning in and of themselves, but are simply features that the brand possesses. In an employment sense, attributes could include everything from a well known logo, a well known CEO, or a visible location to attributes such as the type of employment or job the organisation is best known for and the average age of the workforce. That is, the physical features of the employer brand.

Functional Benefits

These are the consequences of the attributes you possess. Possession of certain attributes gives you the ability to provide a certain set of related functional benefits to your people. For example, if one of your attributes is that you are government-owned, one of your functional benefits may be that you are able to offer above-average stability. If your company has the largest and most dominant customer or tender in the category as an attribute, then a related functional benefit would be the opportunity to work with high-profile

clients or on cutting-edge projects, with obvious attractions in terms of market awareness, stimulating and challenging work, and training and learning opportunities that this would bring.

Emotional Rewards

How do you want employees to feel as a result of working with your company? Do you want them to feel proud? Smart? Technically proficient? Valued? Confident? These are outcomes that you hope are felt by every employee, and the Evangelists are the best place to start. They can give you the best direction as to the core emotional rewards the employer brand offers.

As an interesting aside, the feelings that you think your employees will see as rewarding may not line up with yours, so you would be well advised to seek counsel on this. Remember the example of the crèche mentioned earlier, and my expectation that employees would respond favourably to the pay rise (which they did, albeit in an understated way), whereas they actually felt more empowered by being given the opportunity to be involved in consultations on design.

Values of the Employee

Values are defined in the Oxford dictionary as being 'one's principles or standards, one's judgement of what is valuable or important in life'.

So this is the part of the pyramid where the things that matter to your employees are captured. It's important that we concentrate on understanding our employees' values, because our brand essence must engage with our employees. Thus if we portray the same values in our brand that our employees hold to be dear and true, we will maximise the likelihood of engagement.

This doesn't mean that we can be flippant in relation to our brand values, or that we can change them willy-nilly. By and large, one's set of values are an established, firmly held belief system that are ingrained more or less from birth. They cannot be chopped and changed. It's important therefore that when your company adopts a set of values as your own, that you and your management team can, and do, live up to them.

The final point about values is to make them as insightful as possible. I can't tell you how many CEOs rattled their values off to me straight out of the HR textbook. By the time you've heard the sixteenth CEO telling you that the values of his company are 'honesty, integrity, fun and mutual respect', the eyes are definitely starting to glaze over. Which is not to say that these companies don't value those things – I'm sure they do. But they're right up there with 'we act with integrity' and 'we value our people.' They are all too easily claimed, spoken and written, but not necessarily believed, exemplified

and promoted. Thinking about your values presents the opportunity to avoid the banal platitudes. Instead of regurgitating what you think would be good to say, try to get to the heart of what really drives your people.

Do they hold dear the value of harmony? Would they say they value passion? Do they crave belonging? Is status a key driver?

You can see how much richer those statements are than 'we value our people'. Further, they give you very clear signposts to the things that your staff consider to be important, and therefore how best to interact with them. The way you present your business results to staff who value 'security' might be quite different to the way you deliver the information to those who value 'individualism'.

Personality

The last step in the pyramid before we brainstorm the all-important brand essence is the personality of the employee brand. This is usually a fun exercise, as we seek to assign personality traits to the company. I ask the participants to imagine the employer brand as a person who has just come into the room, or who they've met at a party. How would they describe that person? Are they fun, dynamic, conservative, sincere, extroverted, responsible, self-assured, optimistic? We invariably end up with a long list of personality attributes, and it normally takes some time to whittle the list down to three attributes that everyone agrees on. It's often easier to look at the words in groups of three, rather than debating the

Confirm your aspirations

relative merits of each individual word. The combined effect of the three words that are chosen will provide an insightful range of personality traits for your brand.

Terms like 'contemporary' should be avoided when considering personality traits. Apart from the fact that I have an aversion to the idea of brands ever being seen as contemporary, the word is hideously overused. Great brands, unless they are truly based on modernity, such as fashion brands, generally have values that are timeless, not ever-changing in an attempt to keep up with the times. Would you really describe any of your close friends as having a 'contemporary' personality?

'Capable' and 'competent' are two other words I prefer to avoid. If I was ever told in a performance review that I was performing at a capable or competent level, that would be the signal that it was time for me to leave …

The method of forced thinking I generally use and recommend to complete the pyramid is brainstorming, producing as many words as possible at each level, and then culling down to the three most relevant terms. This gives us as many attributes as we are able to offer, together with the three most relevant functional benefits, emotional rewards, values of employees and personality traits.

At this stage of the journey, it's time to run the 'red flag' test. When you run your

Confirm your aspirations ▶

eye down the pyramid, does it make innate sense to you? Does it reflect where you want your company brand to go? Does it adequately reflect your dreams and aspirations? Is it gutsy? Will it set you on a future course that, with some skill and daring, is able to be successfully navigated? Does it all 'match'? By that, I mean are there any elements that stand out as conflicting, or ill-fitting? If so, go back and address those items.

The other litmus test is the spread of the 'feel' of the brand across the various levels of the pyramid. The wisdom of a strong brand pyramid is not at each level in isolation, but in the combined impression that the brand conveys. And don't over-use key words or phrases. If you feel that confidence is a key

part of the brand that's fine, but avoid putting it in as an emotional reward, a value and a personality attribute! Use your words wisely, grasshopper.

Brand Essence

Once every level of the brand pyramid is complete, it's time for the most important part of the process, that of identifying the brand essence. This is the key step, because it contains the employee value proposition, and embodies the heart and soul of the brand – the DNA of the company, if you will. As stated earlier, a good brand essence has parameters that make sense to people, and is simple, differentiating and above all, true.

Importantly, it is not a slogan. Sometimes people have an irresistible urge to make

their brand essence into something they can print on coffee cups, mousepads and t-shirts. The brand essence isn't supposed to be a sexy statement or a slogan. It is the summation of all that you have reflected in your brand pyramid, the embodiment of your company's spirit.

try to make the brand essence a set of three words, including a noun which describes what the company is, and an adjective describing how it is different. Sometimes these statements sound quite clunky, which is perfectly fine, as long as it reflects the essence of your employer brand.

The final point to bear in mind is that the brand essence should include words that do not appear in the pyramid. Simply

identifying the three words used most frequently throughout your brainstorming session and putting them together to create the brand essence is not what it is about. A true brand essence summarises the intent of the brand, the embodiment of what the company is about.

Most established companies will already have used a tool such as the brand pyramid to determine their external brand.

They will have developed a brand positioning statement along much the same lines as we have discussed here, but aimed at their consumers, rather than their employees. If you have already done this, then you are one step ahead in the development of your employer brand because you have already thought about what your company offer is from an external perspective.

You should generally find that your internal brand essence is not too far away from your external brand essence. This varies wildly by category and line of business, but your internal and external brand personality in particular should be closely aligned. As Virgin Mobile says, 'The way we communicate externally, we sort of have a philosophy of the way you say it is the way you should write it, and that is what we do internally ... there is very little difference between the two'.

The way you say it, is the way you should write it

A case study

Many companies are understandably unwilling to share their corporate intellectual property in relation to how they see their brand with an audience, either externally or internally. However, one of my clients, community services group Melbourne Citymission, recently went through the brand pyramid process, and were happy to share the outcome.

Melbourne Citymission was established by the Churches of Melbourne in 1854 after initially employing six missionaries to work alongside people living in poverty and struggling to survive in the tent cities that sprang up along the Yarra River during the Victorian Gold Rush.

They were established as a non-denominational organisation to provide assistance to thousands of Victorians of many faiths and cultures who are disadvantaged, isolated and vulnerable. The focus of Melbourne Citymission's work is supporting people to take charge of their own lives and participate fully in community life, providing 'a hand up, not a handout'.

Confirm your aspirations ▶

When I first met with the Executive to refine the external core values of the Melbourne Citymission brand, this was the brand pyramid we developed:

Melbourne Citymission Brand Pyramid

The pyramid the Executive constructed that day contained a number of interesting elements. CEO Anne Turley commented that 'This process has been crucial to Melbourne Citymission finding a way to articulate the values we apply to our service practice in a way that corresponds to our external marketplace'. Probably the greatest single use of the tool has been an internal prioritisation of the activities the body has found themselves involved in.

As Communications Manager Eloise Hinckley noted, 'This provides us with a platform to develop and promote who we are to our external stakeholders and challenges us to find new methods

that enable us to communicate to a wider audience than we have been able to reach in the past'.

Once the external brand pyramid was in place and the resulting marketing program underway, I turned my attention to the internal brand. As it stood, Melbourne Citymission had not assessed their internal culture against the brand pyramid, so we gathered the HR and marketing people together and, using the external brand as a road map, created the employer brand pyramid.

This is what it looks like:

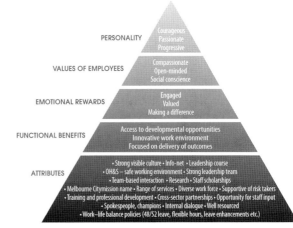

The process revealed some fascinating insights. First, the staff group proved to be in agreement with the Executive, who had fashioned the external representation of the brand. This was no mean feat. The fact that two entirely different groups of people had reached the same outcomes about twelve months apart is testimony

Confirm your aspirations ▶

The process highlights for us the systems and changes required to ensure our workplace and staff feel ... aligned with our external image

to the validity of the process in general, and to the strength of Melbourne Citymission's brand in particular. It may not have been an explicitly stated brand focus, but it appears to have been shared. For many, the process confirmed what was already in their minds.

Second, the staff group changed only those elements of the brand pyramid, within the Attributes and Functional Benefits areas, that they felt were irrelevant. Attributes were changed to reflect the attributes that an employee sees Melbourne Citymission offering, and the Functional Benefits were changed accordingly to reflect what the internal audience believes to be the result of those attributes. The three elements that were chosen are clearly directed at an internal audience, as opposed to the focus of the external brand.

The most profound finding was the agreement between the staff group and the Executive in relation to all other areas of the pyramid. Despite the internal and external brands being aimed, in functional terms, at different audiences, both groups saw the brand as representing the same values. This is a classic example of the alignment of the external and internal brand. Melbourne Citymission's goal is to develop an engaged workforce that is every bit as connected to the brand as external stakeholders, and the brand pyramid process has given them a framework on which they can build the appropriate plans to achieve their goal.

Commenting on the overall process, Communications Manager Eloise Hinckley said, 'We had not thought of applying our external brand pyramid to our internal culture before. The process highlights for

us the systems and changes required to ensure our workplace and staff feel aligned with our external image'.

Brand Personification Tools

As either an adjunct to or an exercise preceding a brand pyramid workshop, I will often use a range of other tools to encourage employers to personify their brand in some way. The three main methods I use are picture clipping, eulogies and brand archetypes.

1. Picture Clipping

Prior to a workshop, I will often send identical copies of women's magazines to all participants and ask them to clip three pictures that they think describe the employer brand as it is currently, and three that describe how they would like the employer brand to be perceived in the future. The pictures are not meant

to be literal depictions of the company, therefore they should not include logos of admired organisations. Further, they do not need to be a specific reflection of the company. Rather, they can be an intuitive reflection of what the company brand means to that individual.

A picture clipping places everyone on the same level. You are not asking people to write a thesis espousing their theory of how they think things should be, but just to respond at a base level about how their brand speaks to them in terms of an unrelated set of images. They invariably have dozens, if not hundreds, of pictures to choose from, so it is fascinating to observe how often people choose the same ones.

A brand personification exercise such as this is more difficult than it sounds, and the results that emerge are fascinating on a number of levels. First, it is interesting to see how much agreement there is around the table, and how united your management team is in their understanding of where the brand is currently positioned.

I once ran this workshop for a company that marketed alcoholic beverages. We were looking at the external depiction of the brand for a particular beverage, and at the typical user of this product. The Managing Director chose a picture of Pierce Brosnan in James Bond mode, the epitome of suave sophistication. However, his Marketing Director chose a picture of an underage female wearing a flannelette shirt. Needless to say, that was one extremely interesting brand essence workshop that soon found itself addressing some pretty core issues!

The second thing that is exposed by the picture clipping exercise is the distance between where the brand currently resides and where the participants want it to go. There is often some contention about where the brand is currently situated, but universal agreement on where they want it to go. The brand pyramid process can help them to work out how they will get there.

The final thing a picture clipping exercise can reveal is sub-conscious attitudes towards elements of a brand. Time and again, I have seen several people in a group choose pictures incorporating straight lines and other expressions of overwhelming rigidity but, up until that point, they haven't expressed any concern about a lack of flexibility in the workplace.

Once a number of people around the table have expressed the same sub-conscious notion, however, it becomes clear where the brand needs to work harder to engage its people. Such is the benefit of 'Forced Focus'.

2. Eulogies

Another exercise I have used successfully as part of a 'Forced Focus' approach to brand personification is encouraging people to eulogise a brand. A bit

weird I know, but bear with me. First, you ask people to pretend that the brand in question is a person who has come to life, and can interact with you on a human level. Then you ask them to express how they would feel if that brand suddenly 'died'.

I ask people to actually write the eulogy for the ex-brand, and then reflect on the emotions they are feeling. I recently conducted a research study for Noodle Box, the Asian noodle chain, and included the eulogy writing exercise in the course of my research. This is one of the responses I received:

'Oh Noodle Box ... I didn't know you for very long, but the time we shared was magical. So tasty, so convenient, and oh, such good service. You always made me feel so special, like I was the only customer, when really your loyalty is spread over the vast region that is Melbourne. There is no substitute. Wednesday nights will never be the same. I only wish you'd lived long enough to share your blessing on an international scale – you had such potential.'

Pretty remarkable, huh? That sounds like a brand that has engaged with their consumer. Even more interesting, however, is the eulogy that I frequently see in employer branding workshops. They generally go something like this, which is from a company that shall remain nameless:

Confirm your aspirations ▶

'It's sad you've passed away – but I'm more worried about me than I am about you. Even though I saw you every day I'm not sure I ever really knew you. You used to talk at me all the time. But I never really felt you were that interested in me. Oh well, I guess I'll miss you, but I'm sure I'll find another friend.'

There's obviously a huge difference between the two eulogies, and it's not hard to see which one reflects the stronger brand engagement. While exercises such as this don't lead to a specific outcome, like the brand pyramid process, they do shed valuable light on where the brand is now, and how it is perceived both internally and externally.

3. Archetypes

One further tool that is becoming increasingly popular is the use of brand archetypes. A brand archetype is basically the personification of the brand essence in such a way that anyone from any culture can instantly recognise and relate to it. Swiss psychiatrist Carl Jung was the inventor of this technique, determining that irrespective of the culture from which the mythology he was studying had originated, there were consistent patterns in the nature of the characters that emerged. Many strategists have expanded the number of characters available since Jung's work, and some now claim to have identified up to 66 possible brand archetypes, including the Explorer, the Ruler and the Innocent.

The Hero and The Outlaw: Building Extraordinary Brands Through the Power of Archetypes, Margaret Mark and Carol S Pearson outline the following twelve archetypes and their primary attributes:

The Innocent:

- Wholesome, pure

- Forgiving, trusting, honest

- Optimistic, enjoy simple pleasures

The Explorer:

- Adventurous, restless, desire excitement

- Independent, self-sufficient

- Values freedom

The Sage:

- Thinker, reflective

- Expert, advisor, teacher

- Confident, in-control, credible

The Hero:

- Warrior, competitive, aggressive, winner

- Principled, idealist, challenge 'wrongs', improve the world

- Proud, brave, courageous, sacrifice for greater good

The Outlaw:

- Rebellious, outrageous, disruptive

- Feared, powerful

- Countercultural, revolutionary, liberated

As brands seek to provide shorthand summaries of what they stand for, archetypes can provide wonderfully rich tapestries for the positioning of a brand. Imagine a brand that is an archetypal Outlaw (think Harley Davidson), Sage (think Oprah) or Caregiver (think Heinz baby food).

Archetypes can be equally applied to employer brands as we seek to determine a brand essence that reflects the truth of the company's values. They can help us to understand the future brand essence, our code of behaviour and our culture. It is clear that a Lover will communicate with staff quite differently to a Hero, right down to the language of engagement they use. In their book

Confirm your aspirations ▶

The Magician:

- Healer, spiritual, holistic, intuitive

- Catalyst for change, charismatic

The Regular Guy/Gal:

- Not pretentious, straight shooter, people-oriented

- Reliable, dependable, practical, down to earth

- Value routines, predictability, the status quo, tradition

The Lover:

- Intimacy, sensuality

- Passionate, seductive,

- Seek pleasure, to indulge, follow emotions

The Jester:

- Clown, jester, trickster

- Playful, take things lightly, create a little fun/chaos

- Impulsive, spontaneous, lives in the moment

The Caregiver:

- Nurturing, compassionate, empathetic

- Supportive, generous, selfless

The Creator:

- Innovative, imaginative, artistic, ambitious

- Experimental, willing to take risks

The Ruler:

- Manager, organiser, 'take charge' attitude

- Efficient, productive

- Confident, responsible, role model

All the ideas contained in this chapter are aimed at helping you to determine your employer brand. Whether you use any or all of them is fairly immaterial – the power of 'Forced Focus' will become evident when you do something to articulate the direction in which you want your brand to go in future. Your employees need something to unite behind, and to follow. If you don't show them the way, they will meander along random paths, and reduce their engagement. Once you strike your future employer brand, it is so much easier to navigate the way.

Which brings us to the next step in the journey – Applying your employer brand.

A goal without a plan is just a wish

Antoine de Saint-Exupery 1900–1944

08

Apply the plan

The same psychologist who told me that people were generally either 'outcome' or 'process' driven went on to tell me that, of course, I was an outcome driven person, with a capital 'O'. Not surprising really for a consultant who actively practices the art of 'Forced Focus' thinking! But I must confess, I also have a certain bias towards process – if only because I have seen so many projects that could have had terrific outcomes fail miserably due to a lack of it!

There is no doubt that this is the hardest step in the journey of building an employer brand. It's very time consuming, it requires a real commitment from the top, it's not terribly sexy, and it's hard to tell if it's actually working. Little wonder then that it generally doesn't get done well. But the stakes are high, because if you can't execute, then all the work you have done to date will be wasted. Sadly, this is not like a Frequent Flyer program, where every step you take earns additional points. You must complete this stage, or else forsake the entire journey.

Corporate Australia does not have a terrific record when it comes to

It must be considered that there is nothing more difficult to carry out nor more doubtful of success, nor more dangerous to handle than to initiate a new order of things. For the reformer has enemies in all those who profit by the old order and only lukewarm defenders in all those who profit by the new order

Niccolo Machiavelli, The Prince

understanding an issue and then implementing a process to address that issue. I asked a number of CEOs why they thought this was so, and many found it difficult to identify any one particular barrier to more effective implementation. Make no mistake, I believe that all the

CEOs interviewed are committed to implementing real change, and some are making more progress than others. But to reiterate, there appears to be a yawning chasm between understanding that there is an issue to be addressed, and possessing the ability to implement a systematic, company-wide program that will lead to real change.

It stands to reason that a chapter on how to actually 'Apply' your employer brand runs a grave risk of simply spouting platitudes about how to implement a project.

After all, the actual steps involved in implementing an employer brand project are no different to the steps necessary to implement any other major project – the same principles apply. Nonetheless, it is worth outlining some key philosophies and action points that companies who have successfully implemented strong employer brands seem to have embraced. In summary, there are four basic aspects of the application process that seem to make the difference between success and failure.

Lead from the top

There are two parts to this point – first, the need to demonstrate leadership, and second, that it must emanate from the top. I mentioned the importance of leadership to employees earlier when discussing the 5 'C's, and in particular Charisma. From a Gen Y perspective in particular, but in fact for all employees, leadership is critical with regard to the application of the employer brand. As a career marketer, one of the more striking findings from my research is that leadership is even more critical to the development of the internal brand than it is to the development of an external brand.

For example, if we look at the values of any well-established traditional brand, customers are often able to surmise those values by observing how the brand behaves, and the consistency of its messages over time. Strong brands have values that are timeless, and the brand is 'bigger' than any one individual. It doesn't matter who the CEO of Coca Cola is – the values of the Coke brand have remained consistent over the years. Generally, a CEO is unable to implement changes that impact on the strength of a well-established brand.

If a 'rogue' CEO showed signs of heading down that path, then the culture of the organisation might well stop their progress and weed them out, or else the customers could revolt and vote with their feet. This would invariably result in a decline in sales leading to the CEO being shown the door pretty quickly before any further damage could be done to the brand. Consumers generally do not respond favourably when a brand they have come to know and love suddenly decides to represent itself as something else – witness disastrous brand extensions such as New Coke in the United States by way of evidence.

One might think this doesn't apply to well-defined external brands that identify closely with a personality, for example Virgin and Richard Branson, but even in cases such as these, a change of CEO would not necessarily prove catastrophic for the external brand. Sure, the next CEO of Virgin will have a tough time trying to live up to Branson's larger than life persona but, by the same token, the culture has been extremely well disseminated, and it is unlikely that whoever gets the job would consider contravening any of their established values. International management consultancy Booz Allen and Hamilton conducted a survey in 2003 which found that the average tenure of a CEO in Australia was 4.4 years, down from 5.8 years in 2001, so it appears companies are turning their CEOs over too quickly to enable them to really make a dent in a strong external brand.

Unfortunately, the same cannot be said of the internal brand. Leadership, and the

the employer brand occurs much more quickly and with a much more direct impact than on the external brand. This is why leadership is so important to the development of a robust employer brand.

I discussed this at length with Peter Sinclair, Director of Sales and Marketing for SCA, where his portfolio includes brands such as Sorbent, Purex and Deeko. Peter's most recent employer before SCA was Fosters

> # You can't wait for inspiration. You have to go after it with a club   Jack London 1876–1916

type of leaders you have in a company, is absolutely critical to the formation and perpetuation of an employer brand. As opposed to a traditional brand, the employer brand values will change with a change in CEO. Ronda Jacobs at Cardinal Health was quite clear about this when she took over: 'I don't want the brand to be the same for employees as it was under the previous CEO. So I don't want the same values that were always there because I don't see value in duplicating them and growing them'. If there is a change in personnel, the flow-on effect on the values, and ultimately

Breweries, and he was classically trained at Procter and Gamble, so he has been exposed to a variety of leadership models. Peter has experienced something of an epiphany in his understanding of what drives employees, and the importance of leadership: 'I think that the name on the door is far, far less important to people than the need to learn and to grow through working with people they respect … a lot of people are far more interested in who they are working with … so it is about individuals as much, if not more so, than it is about organisations'.

This goes to the crux of why people might be attracted to a particular company. In the past, it might have sounded like the sexiest thing ever to work at Nike and, for many, maybe it still does. But the market has matured now, given the 'Forced Focus' of choice. In acknowledgement of the increasing value placed on satisfaction at work and a greater work–life balance, people now identify less with the external brand the company portrays, and want to know more about the internal brand in terms of the individuals who make up that brand as a factor in their choice of employment.

Think about this in relation to your own industry. Whenever you are seeking to hire new people, there will be a few organisations whose people you really rate, and a few you wouldn't hire from if they begged you. What is that based on? Is it just purely on external performance? I doubt it. There are other factors at play in determining your propensity to hire from particular firms.

Peter Sinclair expands on this: 'Take one of my previous employers for example. They were a highly successful company – but the vast majority of people will not look at them and go wow, they made double-digit profit last year and they have for the last three or four, I will go and work there. They will go "Tell me about the company, who is running the joint, how do they operate, what are they like?" Four or five years ago, using

that as an example, people would have said there are good people in there doing good stuff, they are developing people, there is high team morale and they are learning a lot. Now they are going: what a terrible place to work'.

As Peter points out, the external signs of success at a company may be significant, and the brand values they convey for each of the products they make may well remain unchanged or potentially even strengthened, given continued strong economic performance. But the internal brand has deteriorated, and this has had a significant effect on the group's employees and potential employees. It is the difference between the functional and the emotional. Peter again: 'The functional attributes are the same. And I would argue that all of the internal stuff is still the same as well. However, the people who are running the joint and the way in which that impacts the perception of the internal (employer) brand in the market place is significantly different'.

To go fast, go alone. To go far, go together

African Proverb

The implications of this for the 'Apply' stage of the employer branding process are significant. If it is true that a key part of the employer brand is the actual individuals at the top, then those individuals clearly need to demonstrate strong leadership. 'So what's new? Organisations with good leaders at the top have always been better off', I hear you saying.

That may be true, but does your company recruit with a view to obtaining great leaders, or does it recruit based solely on functional job skills? I put this to Peter Sinclair in relation to his own recruitment experience at SCA: 'I've got no doubt that they bought what they believed to be my functional expertise'. But if you ask him where he – and probably the organisation in retrospect – now sees his value, it is both his functional ability and, importantly, his ability to lead an organisation through a period of crisis and transition. Once again, it is clear that while the functional aspects are important, the emotional values are critical.

It was inspiring to discuss this topic with Robin Berry, former Managing Director of adidas in Australia. When he first came to the position, Robin noted that people had in fact been hired by their silos for their ability to perform a functional task: 'You might have got someone who was really good at his line management job but not great at the leadership stuff'.

So how did they balance that against their aspirations? 'We tried to put more processes in place so we could direct their behaviours against their inclinations. When we hired, we tried to hire against those types of competencies. And we started to measure performance by their contribution towards leadership, with a fairly nebulous concept in terms of their KPIs, but looking at the level at which they participated in leadership teams … did they initiate anything? Did we get feedback from them? Did they fight for things they believed in?'

As nebulous as that process might have been, I think it's a good example of consciously trying to recruit and attract not just for the functional silo, as Robin puts it, but for the leadership traits an organisation needs. Robin would look for indicators of potential leadership in the language his people used, and how well they were able to look beyond their silo and have a wider view of life. He didn't want to hear about business results – Robin assumed that if they had a plan that he had signed off on, then they would be capable of implementing that plan successfully. But did they have ideas, vision and purpose? He wanted to ensure that 'they were all looking up, and all looking in the same direction'.

Sandra Blackburn at Pacific Brands in Australia said that her organisation had begun to do the same thing with their potential employees: 'We actually put

The best ideas are common property

Seneca

them through some testing to understand more about their emotional intelligence, so we can build a profile, and have a better understanding of whether they would fit into our culture at Pacific Brands'.

As mentioned earlier, ING Direct recruit on culture first and technical ability second. Their ex-CEO, Vaughn Richtor, achieved legendary status in building a high-performance culture at ING Direct. Sharyn Schultz said of Richtor: 'He was the ultimate iconic leader in that he walked the floor, he knew everyone's name in this building, he knew everyone's name on the floor. He used to just wander up and say hi, what sort of challenges have you got today, and people had the opportunity to talk. This wasn't a token performance, he was genuinely interested. And the people could feel it'.

The development of leaders with a strong EQ (Emotional Quotient) as opposed to IQ (Intelligence Quotient) is a study in itself.

Daniel Goleman popularised the notion of Emotional Intelligence in 1995 in his book Emotional Intelligence: Why it can matter more than IQ. According to Goleman, rational intelligence (IQ) contributes about 20 percent to the factors that determine success in life, whereas EQ is among the factors that contribute 80 percent. Leaders with a high EQ are typically able to unleash people's passions and emotions, thereby bringing greater energy, commitment, integrity and that all-important element engagement to the workplace. They set the tone in terms of morale, and provide the stage for employee feedback and development. In the future, their ability to lead a flat organisation of empowered workers will constitute a critical competitive advantage.

The implication for the 'Apply' step in the process of building an employer brand is that while IQ remains relatively stable throughout life, EQ can be learned and improved. Listening is a huge part of EQ (i.e. empathetic listening, rather than 'I'm nodding at you and thinking about what I'm going to say next' listening). The real test of EQ is whether senior management and the organisation as a whole truly embraces EQ and leadership qualities as an important part of the employer brand process. As noted earlier, there is a penchant for looking at these so-called softer measures as 'nice to do', or 'wank', as opposed to something that is critical to the success of the company. Employees can sniff a lack of genuine commitment by organisations to their people at a hundred paces.

There is no doubt that strong leadership is one of the absolute key aspects of being able to Apply your employer brand within your organisation, both now and in the future. 'Forced Focus' will ensure that leadership is fostered, and we will hopefully see a greater commitment to training in this area.

The second part of the equation is whether that leadership has to emanate from the top, or whether the creation of a valued employer brand can be facilitated by middle or lower management. My belief is that it must be top down – middle and lower management cannot lead the revolution. In an employer branding sense, clearly the leaders of the company are the ultimate custodians of the brand, and they are responsible not only for agreeing on the brand essence, but for living it as well. Middle management, in particular, has a critical role to play in the implementation of the brand essence that senior management or the leadership group has established, but middle management cannot lead the company – it must be top down.

Many CEOs I interviewed identified middle management as the key to whether or not success was achieved. But Gordon Howlett, CEO of Thorn Australia and New

Zealand, notes how critical it is to motivate and inspire the middle management group, rather than expecting them to lead anything in particular: 'I think the biggest difficulty you've got now is you can always sell to the troops, but you've got to convince your key middle management people that it is a worthwhile objective because, after all, they've got to do all the work.' And that's not as easy as it sounds. Gordon goes on to say, 'If I started up a business and I had a choice of ten people, maybe I would be better off having ten Gen Y people, because they think – who is this old fogy … but if you could actually engage them and actually convince them that this is the way we should go and we will have fun and make money, they will do it. And that may be more productive than me talking to people ten years my junior who have been through the mill with me and say, do we really have to do all this again?'

The senior management team at Kennards is grappling with this issue right now. In the past, they have had a very strong employer brand that, despite never being formally documented, is widely recognised. Peter and Andy both display high levels of EQ, but the company has grown to such a size that it is no longer just down to senior management. In the day-to-day business of running a branch, employees need to identify as much with their Branch Manager as they do with senior management. Kennards are actively working on a range of solutions to address this problem, and that puts them a fair way ahead of the pack, many of whom are yet to even recognise these issues in the workplace.

Many large companies face this challenge – indeed, the Defence Force provides a fascinating example of the Command and Control model which is passed efficiently down to the front line. In my opinion, a leadership model that is built from the top down, but has devolved authority at its core, is the best form of management.

Doug Shears agrees that leadership is critical: 'You've got to have a leader who is very visible all the time … It shows that somebody is concerned or interested … and if there is a perception that they are interested and they care, then people commit. No care, no commitment. It makes a big difference'.

Hudson CEO Anne Hatton endorses the 'lead from the top' approach: 'I really believe that it has to start from the top; it can't be built from the bottom up'. She notes that the role of the CEO has changed over time to reflect this trend: 'far more as the leader externally, but also very much the leader internally … you know, bring the idea from within and create, I guess, the vision'.

Jim Collins, formerly a Stanford University academic and the author of *Good to Great: Why Some Companies Make The*

Leap … and Others Don't, found that the most outstanding leaders are not necessarily the extroverted, high-profile leaders exemplified by Richard Branson. Sure, there are some who fit that mould, but many more possess qualities that are more aligned to a process that develops the core values of the company, and ensures that all employees agree with and

> I really believe that it has to start from the top; it can't be built from the bottom up
>
> Anne Hatton, Hudson CEO

adhere to those values. When that occurs, the company is truly visionary and has the best chance of living its chosen employer brand principles. It's kind of hard to do that from middle management.

In summary, the primary factor that determines a company's ability to successfully Apply their employer brand is whether or not they lead from the top. Employees judge with their hearts, not their heads, whether a company is truly united behind a promise.

Play the 'name the company' game with your friends – whether or not you have any direct experience of the brand, you can

Superior communication

Communication – particularly of new information – is a form of learning. With this in mind, I love to recite a 'learning' anecdote I once read in that bible of anecdotes, *Reader's Digest*. A reader was travelling on an aeroplane and was sitting next to a young girl, maybe five years old. The girl was entertaining herself counting backwards from ten to one, in perfect order.

usually agree about which companies you think really live their employer brand essence. Leadership is absolutely crucial here. As Sensis's Group Manager – Customer Marketing, Amanda Duggan, said, 'If you think you are leading a bunch of people and then you look around and there's no-one there, then you're just going for a walk!' An ability to lead from the top – and senior management that displays true leadership – is more important for building an internal employer brand than it is for building an external brand.

The reader was clearly impressed with this feat – quite an achievement for a child her age. So she said to the girl, 'That's very good being able to do that, did you learn that at school?' Matter-of-factly, the little girl replied, 'No, I learnt that off the microwave'.

Children are like that – they learn by rote at a young age. My two boys remind me of this every day. Max, who is three, can recite the entire book *Where The Wild Things Are*, page by page. He knows exactly which words appear on each page, so as he recites the text, it looks like he is actually reading. Of course, he's not really reading – he merely recognises the visual cues and is able to recall the words perfectly.

It's the same with advertising jingles. The boys are able to sing Cadbury's 'wouldn't it be nice if the world was chocolate' jingle at a moment's notice. More disconcertingly, their repertoire also includes Steel and mesh, steel and mesh, forget about the rest, there's one place to go, that's Wolters with an 'O', oi!

Children are able to recite words without making any judgement regarding the meaning of those words. Of course, that all changes when they hit school, and encounter the peer group phenomenon that determines what is cool and what is not. They learn about double standards, that

> ## Think like a wise man but communicate in the language of the people
> William Butler Yeats

sometimes you say what you don't really mean, and sometimes you feel something strongly, but don't express your thoughts. This is the start of a lifelong pattern of learning from experience and judgement, rather than simply through repetition.

It always fascinates me how often, even when communication is a two-way interaction, misunderstanding occurs. I'm not talking about deliberate deception – I'm talking about situations where what one person says and what the other one hears is completely different.

What Penny said

What I thought

For a number of years, I conducted a series of lectures for a certificate course the University of New England was facilitating for the Australian Association of Practice Managers (AAPM). My section of the course focused on marketing and branding, so naturally I included some material on communication. As it turned out, it was especially relevant because most of the people who did these courses were 'front of house' staff who dealt with the public on a daily basis in medical practices. They often commented on how difficult the public could be because they didn't listen to a thing they were told, a fact I noted with some amusement, realising that many of these patients would have been sick or in pain at the time and therefore almost certainly in a less than ideal frame of mind when receiving the information.

I developed an exercise to try to demonstrate this point. At the start of the lecture, I would hand out a illustration like the one adjacent.

I would just hand it out as general paperwork, without referring to it at all. I would then deliver my opening address, outlining what they would be hearing over the next few hours. I would point out that the topic was marketing, but this was not advertising – one was a subset of the other. I would talk about the basic marketing strategy I would be imparting, and about how I would be giving them specific tips and suggestions on how to market their business more effectively.

Now I am supposedly a marketing and communications professional, and I had given this same address many times to lots of people in the same setting. I would like to think that, by now, I knew my target, their thoughts and feelings, their concerns coming into a course like this, and how I fitted into the whole scheme of things. In fact, I put a lot of effort into making my opening address a stellar communication performance, really setting up the sessions that were to follow. When I had concluded my opening address, I would ask them to refer to their sheet.

They would be asked to write in the speech bubble on the left the basic thrust of what I had just said – not the whole thing, chapter and verse, but what they understood to be the essence of my spiel. Opposite this, they had to write the thoughts and opinions that had washed through their mind while I gave my address, whatever the topic.

I would then gather up their sheets and continue with my program. During the morning tea break, I would look at the sheets and, when we resumed, I would use their responses to make a number of points.

First of all, I invariably found that at least half the responses to 'What Penny said' were quite different to what I believed I had said. There I was, a professional communicator, one-on-one with a captive audience who had paid money to be there (therefore it was in their interests to listen attentively, especially as they were going to be examined on this material, and wanted to do well), and yet their version of what I had said was often quite different to mine. Even more disturbing, sometimes I would get a response that was the complete opposite of what I had said. For example, having laboured the point that advertising and marketing were different things, with advertising being a subset of marketing,

You can't build a reputation on what you are going to do

Henry Ford

I got this response: 'Penny is saying that advertising and marketing are the same, and of equal importance'.

I was dumbstruck!

Even more insightful were the responses under 'What I thought'. There was the predictable 'This sounds good, I might be able to use this to grow the practice a bit'. Thank you, Boomers. And there was 'Sounds OK, but will wait and see when she gets to the actual point'. Thank you, Gen Xs. But there were also responses such as 'Geez I'm hungover

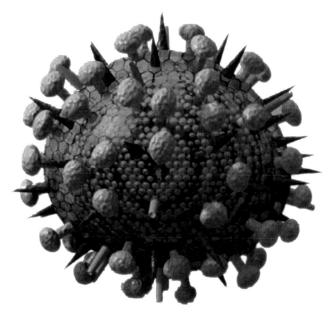

and I need a fag!', and 'I wonder if my kids are OK, I miss them', or better still, 'I like what she's wearing'. These are honest responses (and I thank those people dearly for them) that serve to highlight the challenges of effective communication.

It's clear that even supposed professional communicators, who purport to hold an audience in the palm of their hand, are still at the mercy of the listener in terms of how well their message is taken on board. And so, as I would explain to my AAPM students, is it any wonder that your patients, sick, in pain, worried, confused, or all of the above, don't actually hear what you are saying, despite you telling them very clearly?

So it is with all communication in the workplace. We may think we are communicating clearly and openly, but that doesn't mean our employees see it that way. How often does the rumour mill spring into action in your workplace, with a morsel of overheard information spreading like wildfire, increasingly mutated by the 'Chinese whispers' effect? How often have companies told

152

their staff that everything was 'on track towards achieving our performance targets' on Tuesday morning, only to hand them a pink slip as they've headed out the door on Friday afternoon?

We have seen that workplaces have clearly lost their reputation for trust and loyalty – and that includes trust in what is said. It is the task of every CEO and manager to rebuild that trust. The process must start at the top, be disseminated throughout the organisation, and be instilled into the employer brand. Marcus Blackmore shared a quote from Woodrow Wilson that he often uses: 'The ears of the leader must ring with the voices of the people'.

The final critical factor necessary for superior communication – and this one is crucial for Gen Y in particular – is taking the time to explain why. Gen Y will not follow orders without understanding, or take direction without meaning. A good leader will take the time to explain why – and then even the most recalcitrant of employees can be made to understand the logic behind the action, assuming

of course that there is in fact a logical basis! As Doug Shears says, 'If you can lead them and give them opportunity, they will be with you. And if you can't and you explain why you can't or why you don't think they are capable, then that generally brings about a worthwhile resolution for both parties'.

A penchant for action

My personal consulting style, and the value I bring to clients, is based wholly around the principles of 'Forced Focus'. The hundreds of companies that I've worked with share this thinking. There must be a genuine desire for action, whereby senior management forces a company-wide focus on progress – the sort of stuff that keeps them awake at night, worrying about whether they are in fact moving forward. The desire for action must then be translated into visible signs of action, because actions do indeed speak louder than words. What's more, they must be consistent, and in line with the desired employer brand.

There can be no platform for action if there is no plan to carry out. As noted earlier, the implementation of a good plan depends on good old-fashioned project management, so the disciplines of project management should be used to set the parameters of the employer branding task.

Document the scope, assign responsibility for carriage of the implementation, provide a budget

Apply the plan

and a timeline, delegate key tasks and formalise the reporting. Successful companies approach the employer branding task in a formal fashion – and then monitor their progress. It's important to be tough in relation to the measurement process. More on this in step five, Assess, in the next chapter.

It is all too easy to view a project like this as 'the warm and fuzzy stuff', implying that it is somehow of less importance than projects supposedly focused on the so called 'hard' measures of the business. This attitude, which is sadly all too common, speaks to a fundamental lack of commitment from the top to the process as a whole. Employers who undertake initiatives to develop stronger employee engagement experience enhanced productivity, as outlined in Chapter One. Apart from that, the business world is simply too demanding to have your employees wasting time taking on projects to which you are not genuinely committed. More importantly, every organisation must avoid confusing the mere existence of a plan for your employer brand with the successful implementation of that plan.

I once completed a project for a client who had determined that, among numerous other issues facing their senior management team, their employer brand was weak. They were enthusiastic about improving this and, I think, genuinely wanted to implement real change.

They liked the idea of the Brand Pyramid process, so I was brought in to help shape their employer brand, the latest in a long line of consultants they had engaged.

The day I spent with them was very inspiring, and we made real progress. At the start of the session, all participants were actually in firm agreement, both in relation to where the company was now, and where they wanted it to be. There was a great sense of unison, and we reached an outcome relatively easily. They had a reasonable idea of what their employees wanted, they knew where they wanted to go, they shared the vision among themselves, and they set forth towards the future with a lot of the hard work already behind them.

Fast forward to 12 months later, and the next employee climate survey. Disappointingly, very little had changed. In their frustration, I was held accountable, and hauled back in to explain the lack of progress. Naturally I asked to see what had happened after our session. How had they implemented the results of the employer brand process, and the new brand essence?

Well, they explained, the CEO (who was very supportive of the entire process) had announced it during the regular Friday night drinks with all staff, although not everyone made it to these sessions, and there was generally no follow up in relation to anything that happened at these informal social gatherings. So they sent out a brief email that explained what management had done, and the essence they had arrived at. And let's see now, we asked HR to amend the staff manual to include it in there, didn't we? Yep, that's right, we did that, and that happened ... and then we said we'd talk about it again at the February review ... As the conversation trailed off, they grew increasingly sheepish as the truth began to dawn on them.

Full marks for completing the brand process, but it goes nowhere if there is no implementation of the plan that is developed. If you always do what you've always done, then you'll always get what you've always got! This may sound incredibly trite, but you'd be surprised at the number of senior managers who forget that 'talking' and 'agreeing' does not translate into 'doing' and 'selling'.

Merely holding a brand essence workshop does not an employer brand maketh! You need to develop a penchant for action, and be prepared to be held accountable for actually delivering and communicating change the same way you would in relation to any other project. It gives you no place to hide, and forces you to focus!

So what is the secret of successful implementation? Paul Thompson says, 'There is only one way to do it, and that is to get a formal process that commits to the communication'. Paul goes on to explain that he sees a

It is our choices ... that show what we truly are, far more than our abilities

J K Rowling

Harry Potter and the Chamber of Secrets 1999

clear difference between various sites within the SCA organisation: 'Where sites have a strong process, the culture is always better. Being organised allows you to be more flexible. Being disorganised means you are inflexible'.

Shane Freeman says the same thing in relation to diversity at ANZ, which set targets for gender representation in 2005. Some saw this as an old-fashioned move, and there was plenty of criticism from women in particular, who were concerned that their appointment may be perceived as a token gesture. However Shane points out alternative views: 'First, I've got to say it has created more focus than all of the talking that we had done before that ... and there is something about most human beings, if you set a target for them and as long as they can put some rationale around it ... they actually want to have a go at getting to that target'. Sometimes, forcing the process can result in the achievement of the target!

Medtronic have done exactly the same thing, not just for women, but for key categories of employees they want to attract in greater numbers. Such targets aren't public knowledge, but they are increasingly a focus of recruiters generally. The philosophy is simple, according to Medtronic's Senior Director HR Asia Pacific, Neil Chalker: 'What gets measured gets done', says Neil, and initiatives like goal-setting, together with a range of other talent management systems they utilise ensures that company goals are achieved, rather than just remaining as pipe dreams.

In response to the token gesture issue, Shane Freeman laughs it off, saying 'Business is so tough nowadays that anyone who gets an appointment, whoever, wherever ... they have got there on their own merits. Can you imagine us making an appointment for a job just because it reaches a target? It's unthinkable in this day and age. What about the consequences of failure and what that sets up in people's minds for the future? We can't afford that'.

Clearly, execution is critical to successful implementation of the employer brand process and as Paul Thompson says, 'Actually getting people to make sure you give the manager or executive enough time and making them accountable for delivering means that it gets done'.

I asked Anne Hatton what she thought were the secrets of a CEO who is able to effectively Apply the employer brand. Apart from the usual aspects of intelligence, commitment and enthusiasm, she pinpointed the qualities of certain CEOs who in her opinion are the ones who actually make it happen. Of John McFarlane, CEO of ANZ, she says 'I just think he is amazing – he says all the right things and then he does them, and there are not many who do that'.

Sounds easy, huh? But she's absolutely right. Say the right thing, and then act on your words – behave accordingly. The actions that the leaders of a company undertake are critical in setting the tone and essence of the employer brand. Those actions need to be consistent – and they also need to be visible manifestations of the employer brand essence.

Graeme Wise has a back door in his office that leads straight to the car park, but he never uses it. Every morning, he parks his car, walks past the external door to his office, through the front door of the building into reception and then through the internal offices to his own office. He leaves by the same route every night. This is a tangible example of a culture that, in one simple, unspoken act, displays the values of the employer brand. As Graeme says, 'They actually learn from what you do, so if I am inconsistent in any of my behaviours, or if I am not visibly doing things that are important to reinforce the culture of the organisation, then it won't be embraced'.

Gordon Howlett has a similar view: 'You can't hide, you've got to be out and about. One of the things I guess has been part of my reputation is getting out and about. I have always had the habit that if there is a really big decision that has to be made, you should make the decision in the areas it affects. So, if it is a big deal in Perth, make the point of going to Perth to discuss it, and make the decision there. Of course you could make it in Sydney … but it is far better to be involved with the people at the final step, even if you have made your mind up'.

An interesting aside that I noticed in the course of my research was that some of the behaviours that were most definitive in relation to the employer brand were not those that were spoken about or embraced as desirable behaviours, but those which senior management exhibited publicly that were not representative of the employer brand.

People are much more inclined to discuss and internalise behaviours that are modelled than they are to talk about behaviours that are merely encouraged, so addressing contrary behaviour can be a very effective and striking demonstration of the company's commitment to the employer brand.

As Sharyn Schultz at ING Direct says, this can also act as a powerful leadership tool: 'Even though it is a great place to work, we don't suffer poor performance well. We have got much better at identifying, managing and not putting up with it and I think it makes a big difference. We help our leaders identify what is a high performing team and how to manage accordingly'.

Many companies aim to use the employer branding process to force real cultural change, but until employees see the desired behaviour modelled and can judge management's actions for themselves, an employer brand that has been carefully designed and unveiled with great fanfare to staff remains nothing more than a bunch of words. Which is why the behaviour of the leaders, and in particular the CEO, is so important. The

very minute the CEO or leadership team tolerates behaviour that contravenes the employer brand promise, the entire brand loses focus and the process of employer branding becomes another chapter in the ever-increasing collection of 'stuff' that management says, but their employees do not believe.

Check the temperature and adjust

The final factor that separates those companies that are able to successfully Apply the employer brand is that they continue on to the fifth 'A' – they Assess. Without exception, every successful company has strict measurement and review processes in place that seek not just to confirm or deny, but to provide real learning from which to move forward. The best employer brands learn from their own experiences, check the compass, check the bearings and adjust their course accordingly. More on that in the next chapter.

Who should champion implementation?

The question of who is the custodian of the 'Apply' step in the employer branding process is a vexing one. As I mentioned earlier, I am opposed to the somewhat clinical term 'human resources', but it seems that, for many companies, the natural domain of a process such as employer branding is indeed the HR department. It may be somewhat contentious, but I feel the need to challenge that status quo. You may think I'm biased, but I believe that the custodian of the employer branding process should be the marketing department, rather than HR. Indulge me for a moment if you will.

The marketing department's core competences are supposed to involve the conduct and analysis of independent research to discover what the customers in the market want, understand how the company measures up in comparison to their competitors, and thereby determine where the best opportunities for the company lie. They then need to set realistic objectives for the company, determine what the company can do

to meet the expectations of consumers, and then design a program to enable them to achieve the best outcome.

I would suggest that this process is pretty darn close to the 5 'A's that I use to describe the employer branding process, which is not to say that the marketing department should automatically be the domain of employer branding, but as a default position, it makes more sense to me than the HR department. HR may well be the traditional custodians of internal brand communication and staff policy, including recruitment and hiring, but there is little else in the average HR job specification that suggests that it is more likely to provide the skills required to drive the employer branding process than the marketing department.

Now that may reflect a very traditional view of HR, indeed some of the best HR professionals I know actually think more like a marketing person than some marketing people I know (Avril Henry springs to mind), but the reality is, really outstanding HR people who have the skills necessary to implement what is essentially a branding process are few and far between.

It was heartening to raise this question with many CEOs, and find that some of the best examples of employer branding appear to emerge when HR and marketing work together. Amanda Duggan at Sensis says that although HR are the creators and owners of the 'People Commitment' plank that has been in place at Sensis for some six years, they rely heavily on Marketing to assist in communicating their message.

At Virgin Mobile, the programs are also cross-functional, but all the internal communication is done by Marketing. A marketing representative sits in on all the internal HR meetings, so they have the opportunity to vet the communications to ensure that it is in line with Virgin's brand values. In fact, the 'Big Red Book', which outlines many of the traditional HR issues and was created to help all staff through the recent merger with SIMPlus, was designed and produced with Marketing taking the lead role. HR is still every bit as important as other functions at Virgin Mobile, but consistency of brand communication both internally and externally is, quite rightly, regarded as critical, so Marketing holds sway.

Anne Hatton, CEO of Hudson, says the interest in Hudson's employer branding division is coming primarily from HR, who

> # I can't understand why people are frightened of new ideas. I'm frightened of the old ones
>
> John Cage

saw the value in piloting an employer branding process in the first instance. HR often initiate the process, and then Marketing becomes involved. As Anne says, the CEO then acts as the point of balance, with the HR person at one end and the Marketing person at the other.

Paul Thompson at SCA believes that management have a general responsibility to 'make sure that the values that these people want are consistent with yours'. This reflects a recent Deloitte survey questioning the CEOs and HR Directors of 77 organisations about the stewardship of internal communications. While both groups agreed that it was a key priority for their business, at least half were unable to agree on who should have primary responsibility. If it is unclear who should be responsible, or tagged as the broad responsibility of management in general, will it get done?

In all honesty, I'd have to say that the

absolute key to successful implementation of the employer brand is to make sure that someone is actually held accountable. Then the debate starts as to who that should be. Shared enterprise always worries me, as it often ends up being no-one's core responsibility. Nobody takes control or accountability, and the entire program falls through the cracks. So the first step is to commit to appointing someone to take control. The next step is then to determine who, within your organisation, is best placed to assume that role.

What actions have others taken?

So you've done your brand pyramid process, your senior team is in alignment, your middle management is primed, you're ready to live your focus and you have a plan for the future. What exactly can you implement as evidence of your employer brand? As I have said on numerous occasions, it is not just about the functional aspects that are put in place as evidence of your employer brand focus – it is the resultant emotional bond that employees establish with the employer that speaks most loudly.

What follows is a range of ideas that a number of companies have undertaken to demonstrate their own employment proposition to their employees. It is not an exhaustive list – I have included several ideas from some companies, just one or two from others – and at the end is a list of miscellaneous ideas I've come across in the course of my work and research that can't be attributed to any particular company. These ideas are offered as thought-starters, examples of some really creative and engaging approaches that I believe are worth considering when looking for ways to build that elusive emotional connection between employees and the employer brand.

Virgin Mobile

There are so many things to love about the way Virgin Mobile manages their internal brand that it's tempting to devote an entire chapter to them. 'We put as much effort, although probably not as much money, because it is not as costly, into building our brand internally as we do externally', says Rich Field. The Big Red Book that I mentioned earlier is an interactive, 'living' document to which staff contribute regular updates. My favourite section is 'The Virgin Blessing',

written by a staff member to 'bless' the new offices into which the newly merged company was moving. Blessings aside, many of the ideas that punctuate the employer brand experience at Virgin are similar to those used by other companies, but Virgin-branded. The thing is, they do it consistently, and they do it well.

For example, a day you take off after you've done a lot of long shifts, often termed a mental health day elsewhere, is called a 'V-day'. Then there are the Ripper Awards, $25 gift vouchers that recognise a good ad hoc idea provided by anyone, anywhere in the Group. The Mad Virgin Awards are held every quarter, and involve peer-nomination. These are substantial gift vouchers, and all quarterly winners are in the running for the title of Mad Virgin of the Year (now there's a line you don't see on many CVs), the winner of which receives a trip to the UK and a stint in Virgin's UK office. There's a Rhodes scholarship program, whereby employees can do an exchange and spend three weeks in another Virgin company, and there's a range of internal benefits that provide discounted restaurant meals, Virgin Blue flights, etc. Team building and fun are constant themes, with plenty of spontaneous get-togethers where staff can mingle and have a few drinks. These are initiated by the CEO, who takes a lead role in cultivating the desired sense of the brand.

Quarterly reviews are all designed around themes, and the management team addresses the staff on business results and implications while in costume. Statements like 'If Virgin sold socks they would sell them in pairs of three because one always gets lost in the wash' are pasted all over the walls, and they are ceaseless in their promotion of the Virgin way of thinking. At sponsored events, they always involve a lot more staff than is strictly necessary, rostering them on for maybe four hours so they get the chance to spend some time enjoying the event.

As Rich Field says, 'The bottom line is, we get our 300-odd staff to be brand advocates. And every one of them has ten mates who they will talk to. And so it goes. There is a commercial benefit'.

Rich estimates they would spend the equivalent of a full time employee's salary just doing internal event planning, rewards, recognition, internal communication, and so on. It may be spread over a number of people – but a lot of effort goes into it. 'Everything we do we try to keep within the brand context and we do actively promote', he says. Walking around the Virgin offices, you can feel the pulsing heart of a strong employer brand. It made me want to apply for a job there!

ANZ Bank

ANZ is a particularly fascinating example, because banks have long been a prime target for customer angst. It was genuinely refreshing to see statistics indicating consistently less than average turnover, and I was keen to find out more.

I believe that there are three key factors that ANZ really get right internally. The first is one to which Anne Hatton at Hudson alluded, and that is leadership. John McFarlane is clearly an inspirational leader who is widely respected by his peers for not just talking the talk, but for living it as well. As Shane Freeman says, 'The people stuff needs to feel real and accessible, not just something on a plaque or on the Internet'. John McFarlane clearly plays his part in ensuring that occurs – from the top down.

Secondly, ANZ run a unique program called Breakout that was purpose built for them by McKinsey. Indeed, such is their dedication to the scheme that Shane's business card announces him as Group Manager of Breakout. Clearly, Breakout is more than just a passing phase and more than a program – it is what ANZ refer to as 'our culture change process'.

This process is underpinned by a two to three-day Breakout training program that focuses on personal development, behaviour management and communication. It provides three benefits – first, it demonstrates to the staff that senior management is interested in their personal development. Breakout represents a significant investment by the organisation – 20,000 people have been through the program during the five years it has been running. That's an enormous commitment, by any standards.

As Shane points out, 'Most people would get completely bored by the 3000th person and go and do something different'. But it is to their credit that ANZ's management team have continued to apply Breakout with unwavering consistency of purpose and clarity of vision.

Second, Breakout has given staff a shared framework and language for interaction in the workplace. A key component in building a strong employer brand is establishing consistency in terms of language and expectations. The use of a formalised training framework like Breakout is a very positive step in this regard.

Finally, probably the greatest benefit of the Breakout program is the personal development that all employees, but in particular our Gen Y friends, crave. As Shane points out, 'Many people have never had this sort of experience where they learn so much about themselves … I just got another note this morning from someone, people get really charged about it'.

The internal research undertaken by ANZ repeatedly throws up terms like 'caring', 'support', 'individual improvement', and 'self development' as perceived benefits of working at ANZ, and I have no doubt that this is largely due to Breakout. Shane summarises this by stating that 'People feel that people matter'.

The third thing ANZ get right is that they understand the first 'C' – Conditions. As Shane says, 'We have taken the responsibility of making sure our staff are well paid within the context of the market that is occurring, with regular adjustments, and made sure that the conditions under which they are employed are attractive to them'. They have done this over five years, without needing to resort to formal negotiations. Quite frankly, that could not have been achieved in an environment where staff did not trust management, or in a climate of insecurity. It is well known

Apply the plan ▶

that John McFarlane strives to avoid retrenchment at all costs, and Shane must approve any retrenchment in the management group, which totals some 7000 people. As he says, 'I would like to re-install more of this sense of security. It is hard for people to feel that they want to contribute their best if they feel insecure'.

ANZ have certainly managed to achieve business success, both externally and internally, and it appears their employer brand is providing something of a competitive advantage.

The Body Shop

Social responsibility was one of the key elements in the genesis of The Body Shop's brand, and remains a core part of what the brand is about today. Everyone in the company receives two days paid leave to work on a community project of their choice, which can either be undertaken as a group (for which the company will hire a bus to enable a group of staff to do a tree planting program, for example) or individually. Participation is not compulsory, but it forms part of everyone's performance appraisal, helping to build a strong culture, and reinforcing the importance of such projects. They also run an external campaign every year, and are currently into the third year of their campaign against domestic violence.

Managing Director Graeme Wise was instrumental in setting up *The Big Issue*, a community newspaper which aims to

provide homeless people with a way to earn a legal income, while providing an example of a socially responsible business and an alternative to conventional charity as a response to the problem of homelessness. Then there's the First Australian Business mentoring program, which provides business mentoring support to Indigenous small businesses.

Graeme's latest project is Bizness Babes, which works with young women to help them get their businesses established. Young women receive intensive training and the opportunity to get into the workforce and maybe build some innovative new businesses. As Graeme says, 'Even if they don't ever start a business, they will be capable of earning a bit more money'.

These are outstanding examples of caring about people's lives and circumstances, driven by the CEO, which must be a source of considerable employee pride, and serve to reinforce the employer brand. It's hard not to be impressed by such outstanding examples that so truly reflect the employer brand values of The Body Shop.

Visa

Apart from the range of functional employee benefits that many companies now provide, such as free fruit, Pilates classes, mental health days, etc., I was astounded to hear that Visa Australia has enough stock of Tamiflu in their fridges right now to service their staff and families should the Asian Bird Flu Virus take hold. This takes the concept of caring for your staff to a whole new level, and is an impressive example of innovative thinking.

Kodak

I found Kodak fascinating, not because of their shedding of so many jobs, but by the way they managed the process. Management did a huge amount of work trying to help those who lost their jobs to find alternative employment. They paid companies to come in and help employees write resumés, they held an Open Day involving more than 25 other companies spruiking their opportunities on site at Coburg, they advertised those companies, and encouraged the retrenched employees to consider them. They worked very hard to place as much power as they could into the hands of those who felt most powerless, those who were losing their jobs, to enable them to maintain their personal dignity, and at least a modicum of control over their destiny.

These efforts speak volumes about the company's degree of commitment to employees at an extremely difficult and emotional time. Kodak continued to impress, even after their relocation. As Greg McKibbin explained to me, when they were at Coburg, employees had free car parking, a canteen, a medical centre, a fit deck, and a credit union. Many had their own offices, and there was a lot of space. Then they shed some 600 jobs and moved to premises where there weren't enough car parks for everyone, there was no canteen, no credit union, no fit deck, and there were only eight individual offices in the entire building, the rest being open plan.

Now I'd challenge the world's best managers to go through a transition like that, incorporating major changes in virtually every facet of the business, and yet in the course of the relocation, they didn't lose one person. As Greg said, 'We can quite categorically say that not one individual has come in and said, I'm sorry, I can't work here any more because it is not possible for me to get here'. The key seems to lie in the exceptional internal communication that took place throughout the process, with management even providing a guide to the boundaries of the areas they were considering when they first started to search for a new location. 'We tried hard to communicate with them, and we are still trying very hard to make sure that everybody is on board, that everybody understands where the company is trying to get to ... to be honest with them, tell them where we are trying to get to, get them involved in the process, get them involved in the solution', says Greg.

Hudson

You'd expect a recruitment company to be the master of internal brand management – but I guess you're familiar with the concept of the builder living in the worst house in the street. Sometimes, you focus so much on your external business that you lose sight of your internal requirements.

It was refreshing therefore to see that Hudson does indeed offer functional employee benefits such as flexibility packages for workers covering everything from parental leave to younger workers who are seeking flexible hours to study or simply create the balance in their lives they are seeking. Hudson is about to launch a corporate responsibility program that reflects the company's commitment to working with organisations to assist with learning.

Employees will be given a day off to work with others – for example, to teach young unemployed people how to prepare their resumés or how to present themselves favourably at a job interview. So not only is it providing a community service, it is focused on one of the key tenets of the Hudson employer brand, that of learning and development.

Cisco Systems

It would be nigh on impossible to write a book about employer branding without mentioning the United States-based company Cisco Systems. In the late 1990s, Cisco grew from an obscure hardware company to one of the most talked-about and benchmarked firms in the world. They engaged a team of world-class HR professionals to help them build a range of people practices that really resonated with their employees, and they also made a concerted effort to get people talking about them as an employer of choice, further enhancing their employer brand status.

There are simply too many programs that Cisco undertakes in building their employee brand to list them all, but some of the better initiatives include:

- Specific HR policies that focus on Equal Opportunities for ethnic minorities, women, people with disabilities, and Vietnam veterans regardless of race, colour, religion, gender, sexual orientation, age, disability or nationality

- Cisco University, running a blend of interactive classroom and online courses giving employees the ability to study when it suits them. Over 4000 courses are offered and around 70,000 registrations are received each quarter, which represents an average of two per employee

- Employee Assistance programs that offer web-based resources on wellbeing, mental health, depression, alcohol abuse, etc.

- An employee discount program

- Childcare Service at the San Jose campus that looks after more than 400 children

- Parental Support, including mothers' rooms for breastfeeding, and adoption support (a US$2,500 subsidy to help Cisco employees cope with adoption costs)

- Fitness Centres

- Weight Watchers classes, financial planning, on-site dental care for all employees and dependents, on-site haircuts, dry-cleaning, car oil change and car detailing

- Leading the way in the US in terms of companies working to improve accessibility to people with disabilities

Kennards Hire

Kennards spend considerable time and money on recognising employee achievements. For many years, they have supported a Quality of Operations award system that sees every employee invited to an all-expenses-paid dinner in each state to celebrate company successes. Outstanding performances are noted, rewarded and celebrated, and this practice is seen as an important part of the culture. Winners not only receive cash and recognition, but also a trip overseas to keep abreast of what the best companies are doing around the world.

Kennards also conducts numerous comprehensive internal training courses on everything from customer service and telephone selling technique to leadership. Their standard of training and resultant excellence is well-respected within the industry.

One of the more famous examples of promoting employee engagement came after a particularly profitable year. Andy Kennard decided to give one million dollars to his staff, calling it the 'Thanks a Million' campaign. Andy and Managing Director Peter Lancken decided that they wanted everyone to receive an equal share, and that the payment should be made by way of a cheque that went to the employee's home, so their families could also share in the excitement.

Each employee received over $3000 pre tax ($500 for casuals), so you can imagine the excitement for employees who were earning $22,000 per annum. That was some bonus! The cheques were personally signed by Andy and Peter, and were accompanied

by appropriately drafted letters of thanks. The result was astounding.

There was a huge outpouring of thanks from employees, and the company made the national news when a few grateful staff members rang the media to nominate Andy as Australia's best boss for giving away a million dollars to his staff.

Do you know what the best thing was about this gesture? It was heartfelt. I happened to be present at the Board meetings where the initiative was discussed, and at no stage was there any mention of a potential benefit for Kennards through publicity. It was purely and simply a genuine expression of thanks to the staff for their hard work – and it was received as such. As you can imagine, it sent a very clear message about the employer brand at Kennards.

ING Direct

ING Direct burst onto the Hewitt Best Employer list in 2005 with a great performance for a company that was less than ten years old. Sharyn Schultz explained that she was impressed not so much with what the company does, which is not all that different to what the traditional banks do in functional terms, but with how they do it. They certainly seem to live by the cultural values that they espouse, and their relatively low turnover, given that the average age of their employees is 30, tends to suggest that they are getting it right.

Probably the most outstanding feature I see with ING Direct is their real and obvious focus on improvement, which is understandably easier for a younger company that doesn't carry as much baggage as an older one. This extends to their commitment to improvement in terms of their relationship with their people.

The culture actively breeds employee engagement, and they are always prepared to listen and act. The organisation is full of the visible examples of such a culture, and it exudes their employer brand.

Medtronic

Medtronic is also on the Hewitt Best Employer list in Australia, but has an even more impressive claim to fame, having made the US Fortune 100 best employers list in eight of the last nine years. I have already spoken about their mission statement, which remains unchanged since it was written by the founder of the company over 60 years ago. Medtronic have introduced a range of talent management initiatives such as paid maternity leave, and while this is no different to the offering of many companies now, the fact that they introduced it some time ago is testimony to their performance in really living their vision of recognising their people.

Another program that has been in place for some time is called Total Wellbeing. This program provides a considerable range of benefits that exemplify Medtronic's commitment to the individual employee. Part of the thinking behind Total Wellbeing, as described by Neil Chalker, is that 'If people are taken care of, they cease to be concerned about compensation and start to focus on the achievement of the mission'. Taking care of people is an important plank for Medtronic, and one that they find pays consistent dividends in terms of employee engagement.

A final note on Medtronic relates to our shared interest in 'Forced Focus'. As noted earlier, they believe that what gets measured gets done, so they measure all sorts of staff achievements and engagement mechanisms, from the number of high-performing women in the organisation to the number of patents they have achieved in the market. They force themselves to focus on measuring the hard-to-measure aspects to ensure that they actually get done. This is a living, breathing example of the success of 'Forced Focus' thinking.

Blackmores

Another successful company in terms of the Hewitt survey is Blackmores. In pursuing Marcus Blackmore's roadmap of People, Product and Passion, Blackmores have introduced a range of initiatives to engage employees. As an example of

the underlying philosophy, Marcus rarely recognises employees on their departure from the company. He prefers to celebrate their decision to join the company, so every employee receives a gift including an 'A-Z Get Well Encyclopaedia' and Blackmores products with a welcome note when they commence, and a bottle of champagne on every anniversary thereafter. They also receive an after-tax bonus of $1500 to recognise their tenth anniversary with one condition – it has to be spent on the individual. This is an interesting point, because the bonus used to be in the form of a specially designed and crafted diamond-encrusted brooch. Marcus had a vision whereby every employee who chalked up ten years of service would take pride in qualifying for membership of the ten-year club,

with the brooch serving as the symbol of their status. It is testimony to Marcus's leadership that when some of the employees revolted against the brooch idea, preferring to receive something more useful (like a fridge!), he magnanimously gave up his vision and let the concept, to use his words, 'go out the door … you have to think more of them than of you'.

Blackmores believes in sharing their profits, so every six months they divide ten percent of their after-tax profit among staff in proportion to their salaries. They make the announcement a formal affair, during which the CFO explains the results, which provides the opportunity to explain something of the business of doing business to the employees. In 2005, Blackmores paid the equivalent of about four weeks extra pay to each employee through their profit-sharing scheme.

Marcus is a firm believer in the importance of spontaneity in business. Only a few weeks prior to our interview, the Board gave 50 shares in the company to every employee. This wasn't of huge significance in financial terms, but it was totally unexpected, and therefore an important and memorable gesture. As Marcus says, 'I think it is about doing the unexpected'.

Once a month the employees get together in each state to hear the latest company news. If there is a critical event or project Blackmores will ramp up the communication through smaller company-wide sessions. In their head office there is an inviting staff café serving high quality healthy food – naturally. Employees are encouraged to mix and meet there. It appears to be the hub of the company and an informal area where information is shared and traditional functional silos are quickly broken down. When you enter Blackmores it is the 'front door' for many, who often comment on the wonderful vibe that reflects the tone of the entire company.

Marcus is proud that Blackmores was one of the first Australian companies to introduce superannuation to the factory floor. He has a strong commitment to the future of his workforce, and this is reflected in other facets such as his policy in relation to sick and continuance pay. They insure every worker for salary continuance, so if employees get really sick, they receive their full salary for three months, and then salary continuance for up to five years if necessary which, depending on the nature of the illness, may be for life. He cites the example of one employee, a single parent who lived in rented housing with her young son, who was diagnosed with cancer. She had used up all her sick leave, but the Board decided to continue paying her full pay so she could concentrate on getting herself well, no matter how long that took. Marcus recalls the reaction: 'That message got around the company like wildfire. They still talk about it, even though it must have been 20 years ago. I quote

that as an example because if we say we want trust from you, lets demonstrate that trust back to our employees'.

Blackmores also have the usual award and recognition schemes, and quite generous ones at that. These are bestowed on individuals at celebrations that are deemed to be of such importance that the entire company is required to stop work to participate in them. He is proud of his employees' commitment to giving, and explained a scheme they have introduced whereby the company matches employees' contributions to the charity of their choice. For most employees, the commitment is half of a percent of their salary, but whatever it is, Blackmores is happy to match it.

And finally, as a healthcare products company, their commitment to an overall focus on employee health and wellbeing is pivotal. They were one of the first Australian companies to install an on-site gym, not just a bunch of machines in a spare room, but a professionally managed centre with qualified trainers. The new plant Blackmores is building will incorporate a Wellness Centre that will include a lap pool, and visiting practitioners for staff to consult in relation to their health and wellness needs, all subsidised by the company.

Ikea

A similar gesture to Blackmores' profit-sharing scheme was undertaken by Ikea, who shared the total receipts from one day of trading among their employees as a bonus.

Southwest Airlines

In 2005, Southwest Airlines in the United States announced its 32nd consecutive year of profitability, unprecedented in the airline industry, and especially notable given the tempestuous years since the events of September 11, 2001. They are consistently recognised for their external performance in terms of customer service, but I am equally impressed with their internal brand commitment:

The Mission of Southwest Airlines
The mission of Southwest Airlines is dedication to the highest quality of Customer Service delivered with a sense of warmth, friendliness, individual pride, and Company Spirit.

Their mission statement then continues:

To Our Employees
We are committed to provide our Employees a stable work environment with equal opportunity for learning and personal growth. Creativity and innovation are encouraged for improving the effectiveness of Southwest Airlines. Above all, Employees will be provided the same concern, respect, and caring attitude within the organisation that they are expected to share externally with every Southwest Customer.

Now as I have stated repeatedly, it's not enough to just claim that you do these things – you must actually live your essence. The various actions of Southwest indicate that this is indeed what happens there. From their community service angle (their 2005 marketing conference was held in New Orleans, where staff spent significant time contributing to the hurricane relief efforts) to their highly publicised commitment to employees over customers, they worked out long ago the benefits of maximising employee engagement.

Miscellaneous Ideas

- In industries where people routinely work late into the night, many companies provide a meal for people required to work beyond 7.30pm, and a car to take them home if they are required to work beyond 8pm.

- Many companies make spontaneous rewards compulsory, which sounds like an oxymoron, but means that managers are encouraged to hand out thank you notes, gifts or vouchers for movies, books or music on a regular basis as rewards for staff. At our crèche, we have recently included $13 per employee per month in the budget for this purpose.

- A trip to a health resort for workers who, for example, have put in particularly long hours on a major project.

- Allowing employees to bring their dogs to work.

- Employee-organised events such as charity days, picnics, Christmas parties for the under-privileged, etc., sponsored by the employer.

- Sponsoring employees to train or rehearse for events such as the Olympics, or performances in the Arts.

It is a bad plan that admits
of no modification

Publilius Syrus (circa 100 BC)

09

Assess your progress

The final 'A' in the 5 'A's of employer branding is probably the most important in terms of the success or otherwise of the overall process. If you assess the characteristics of those companies with strong employer brands (as we will later in this chapter), one of the common factors is the consistent application of a rigorous and honest monitoring scheme. The key to the fifth 'A' however is to not only assess the results of your efforts, but to be prepared to then implement changes on the basis of that assessment in an effort to continuously improve the process.

Employee surveys

The first question then is, how do you assess the impact of your efforts to engage your employees? And the answer is – you ask them! Most organisations have some sort of employee survey in place, and if you aren't doing this on a regular basis, you should certainly think about it. Employee surveys can help in two ways.

First, as noted earlier in relation to the second 'A', the Audit, they are extremely useful in helping you to find out what people actually want. It is interesting to discover how useful such surveys can

be. Marcus Blackmore cited an example whereby one of his directors encouraged the staff at Blackmores to complete a climate survey. As Marcus explains, 'I am against those things. I think management should have enough communication and interaction with their staff to have the trust of the people to tell them the things that are wrong. Anyway, I have to say that when the climate survey came out, there were a whole lot of things that were wrong, so then you get the opportunity to address them, and we've been doing that. The end result was that we kept using the climate survey. I'm very proud of that'.

So there you go – a doubter who was converted into an enthusiastic supporter of the formal measurement process.

My preference is the use of a combination of focus groups and surveys. Surveys can give you useful responses to broad questions such as overall awareness of a certain policy, or strength of agreement with a specific aspect of the company's culture, but they rarely explain the 'why' behind the responses. It is vitally important to understand the reasons behind people's responses. Good qualitative research isn't just a matter of yes or no, good or not so good – it should offer diagnostics outlining the 'how' and 'why' so you can begin to craft an appropriate strategy to address the issues or concerns that emerge. It's hard to determine how best to address a problem if all you know is how many people agree that the issue is definitely a problem.

Kennards have been undertaking regular staff surveys for many years and some of the responses, most notably in relation to rewards for weekend work, have been fairly consistently negative over that time. The Board had extensive discussions about how best to address this issue but, for a long time, the issue for them was that they didn't really know exactly what the complaint was based on. They knew it was a consistent problem, but they didn't know why, and therefore were finding it hard to craft the most appropriate response. It transpired that the staff were in fact being compensated for weekend work but, because it was rolled into their overall package, some staff obviously weren't aware of this. Others realised that weekend work was being recognised, but felt that the rate of pay was too low.

Once they undertook some focus groups with staff to pinpoint the exact nature of the issue, it was much easier for management to develop meaningful solutions. A new remuneration package has now been designed and implemented, and they are looking forward to seeing the results in the coming months.

Secondly, employee surveys help us to monitor the mood of the people, and whether or not the company and employee behaviour is reflective of the employer brand essence. For example, if your brand essence is Melbourne Citymission's courageous social change-agent, it creates certain expectations in terms of staff behaviour. One would expect that an interaction with the organisation would demonstrate those attitudes quiet strongly, and every time an employee fails to respond in a manner consistent with the brand essence the sense of the external brand is diminished.

But it also sets up some expectations in terms of senior management's behaviour towards employees with regard to the internal brand. If an employee, acting on their own initiative, undertakes a potentially damaging action, then senior management must respond in a way that is seen to be consistent with the brand essence. The development and maintenance of a brand essence is a team effort and a two-way street, and everyone must make a commitment to live by its principles.

So how do you assess degree of coherence between leadership behaviour and brand essence? Robin Berry at adidas confessed that he relied largely on a gut-feel approach to measuring the progress of his senior management team in demonstrating the leadership behaviour to which he aspired. In all truth, this probably worked quite well, but it would only have worked well if Robin was scrupulously honest and consistent with his assessments of all his staff.

If you seek greater certainty, there are numerous external companies who can implement the sort of surveys I am referring to here. Visa use the Gallup Consulting Q12 Employee Engagement process, and Bruce Mansfield finds it extremely useful in monitoring how Visa is tracking. Q12 is basically a set of 12 key questions that Gallup has developed to measure employee engagement and link to business outcomes such as retention, productivity, profitability and so on. Reading through their questions, it becomes apparent that there is a connection with the 5 'C's we know employees want from their workplace. Gallup's Q12 measures the aspects that employees can actually influence, and benchmarks the results based on worldwide responses.

This approach is clearly in contrast with that taken by Robin Berry, and certainly they are on a different scale, but the final point to be made on surveys such as these is to highlight the value of the process itself. As has been noted frequently throughout this book, the concept of 'Forced Focus' is to generate voluntary dialogue and consideration of issues before they are forced upon us. The very process of discussing questions such as those posed in Q12, or any raft of relevant questions for that matter, provides real value for employers. It fosters dialogue, airs issues, highlights weaknesses, and signposts opportunities for change. The answers to

the questions are not ends in themselves. It is the fact that the organisation is forced to focus that provides the means to an extremely valuable end.

If you think back to the different types of employees that were discussed in Chapter Five (Evangelists, Uncommitted and Disengaged), it stands to reason they will respond quite differently in both surveys and focus groups. Evangelists may even go as far as setting up a blog to showcase the company experience, as Heather Leigh, the Marketing Director at Microsoft, has done. Heather's blog is a fascinating read, and does more than any statement that the company might make in their annual report to suggest that Microsoft would be a good place to work.

Of course, it helps that she understands marketing, but in her blog on employer branding she makes the point that 'While my co-workers might tease me for wearing my Microsoft security card when we go out for lunch, I think of myself as a walking, talking representation of our employer brand. And the degree to which I am friendly to the waiter, and even the fact that I take a lunch break is a positive portrayal of Microsoft's employer brand'. Such is the power of company Evangelists!

She continues by discussing the impact of her blog: 'This blog provides a human face to staffing at Microsoft ... people are surprised that we are nice, helpful, care about their careers and that we aren't computer-generated. And while all this blogging has a positive impact on the Microsoft brand, I see an especially profound impact on our employer brand'.

Absolutely – it worked on me. I'd definitely be seeking an interview at Microsoft if that was my chosen field!

A company doesn't just have to limit its surveys to existing employees, either. They also have the opportunity to question potential candidates for employment, for example through interaction on their web site, or simply by cold canvassing. In fact, we are starting to see a very specific promotion strategy for employer branding that has the sole purpose of presenting the brand as an employer of choice, in an effort to attract more than the fair share of available talent. The Fortune 500 Employer of Choice survey is a hotly-contested battleground and many employers are hiring accomplished public relations firms to help position their wares in the most attractive light.

I have also spoken about the use of exit surveys when staff, particularly the Uncommitteds, leave the organisation. You certainly don't want to see some of the factors that have been identified in this book cited as reasons for leaving the organisation. For example, if an employee says they are leaving because the training or culture is unsatisfactory, that should send a fairly loud message to the senior management team that there are some important issues that need to be discussed.

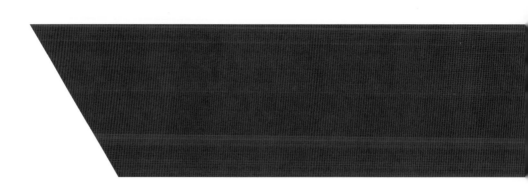

It is to be expected that a wide range of responses will be provided by employees in any survey or focus group. Therefore, it is important to ensure that if it isn't possible to include all staff, a representative cross section of all parts of the organisation is chosen. Employee surveys can provide a powerful lead tool in addressing the fifth 'A', Assessing your employer brand but, as noted in the first 'A', Analyse, it's important to first determine who you want to talk to, and what you want to know.

Characteristics of companies with strong employer brands

The Watson Wyatt Human Capital Index (HCI) studies undertaken in Europe, Asia and North America demonstrate the link between human resources practices and business performance. The HCI has revealed specific bottom line improvements enjoyed by companies who have strong employer brands, such as:

- Clear rewards and accountability – a 16.5 percent to 21.5 percent increase associated with practices such as paying above the market and effective performance management.

- Excellence in recruitment and retention – a 5.4 percent to 14.6 percent increase due to a positive employer brand and focus on skills retention.

- A collegial, flexible workplace – a 9 percent to 21.5 percent increase through practices such as those whereby employees have input into how work gets done, and a lack of workplace hierarchy.

- Communications integrity – a 2.6 percent to 7.1 percent increase through practices that make effective use of employee surveys and sharing of company data with employees.

One of the key characteristics of a Best Employer then is the quality of line managers ...

As the Global Director of Watson Wyatt says, 'Great people management travels well, and it is a true source of competitive advantage'.

Closer to home, global human resources firm Hewitt conducts an annual Best Employer study in Australia and New Zealand. This consists of an employee engagement tool which collects data from employees (similar to Q12), a CEO questionnaire, and what they call the People Practices Inventory (PPI), which is a detailed inventory of an organisation's people practices. The data, the source of which is unable to be identified, is assessed by an independent judging panel. In 2005, 160 organisations participated in the survey, yielding over 40,000 employee questionnaires – a significant and robust sample.

Just because something doesn't do what you planned it to do doesn't mean it's useless

Thomas A Edison

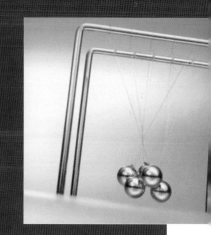

The top companies typically have much lower rates of employee turnover. Data from the 2005 study shows that the average voluntary turnover at Best Employers is 11.4 percent per annum, compared with 15 percent at other companies.

The top companies spend a considerable amount of time recognising and celebrating results. Staff are routinely consulted before decisions affecting them are made. These organisations also tend to have strong performance management systems and linked reward processes in place. Goals are seen to be challenging, yet achievable. Best Employers are twice as likely to encourage employees to set their own goals with their direct manager, rather than having their goals set by the organisation, with individuals having little say in the development of those goals.

Another interesting finding of the Hewitt survey is the difference between large and small companies. With the sole exception of American Express (who have over 2600 employees), all the leading companies in the Hewitt survey have less than 1000 employees, and most have less than 500. In total, of the companies that took part, 13 of them had more than 3000 employees, so it seems that this bias is a natural one, rather than statistically skewed.

It is consistent with trends identified earlier whereby large employers are having to work very hard to engage staff, and are increasingly losing the battle in comparison with smaller companies.

One of the key characteristics of a Best Employer is the quality of their line managers, and the training and development that is provided by the organisation to support them in their roles. Clearly, once you grow to a decent size, it becomes impossible for the CEO to maintain intimate contact with all staff, so it is important that senior management can step up to maintain those engagement practices.

Another key characteristic of a Hewitt Best Employer is the sense that employers care about their staff's careers and their rate of progress. These employers have HR practices that are flexible and adaptable and have their people's interests as the central focus. Employees get to have a say in how they make work fit in with their individual needs, and they also come to understand how their role fits in with the goals of the entire organisation.

In summary, Hewitt has identified five key factors that engage employees, resulting in competitive advantage for those organisations that:

1. Have highly committed, visible leaders who truly believe in their people

2. Clearly articulate what they stand for, and their brand promise to employees

3. Connect their people with their internal organisational strategy

4. Inspire and motivate a high performance culture

5. Align their people practices with organisational objectives

Once more, these five practices are completely in line with the 5 'C's, and go a long way towards explaining why these companies have such strong employer brands. Generally, the processes underlying these five key attributes are more deeply embedded into the organisational psyche of the leading companies, and structured processes are in place to ensure that implementation occurs. Once again, this points to the importance of leadership from the top in

establishing this culture of engagement, and ensuring that the processes and expectations are clear and accountable.

How else can you tell if it's working?

Apart from the raft of empirical evidence one can gather about one's employer brand from ongoing measurement, there are a range of qualitative, gut-feel questions that the senior management team can ask itself to track performance. Some measurements that companies might consider include:

- How easy is it to attract talent once you've found it? If it is proving consistently difficult, and you're more often that not receiving a negative response, you might want to conduct some more empirical research to determine what's going on.

- How good is the public relations commentary about your company? Do you get talked up? Shane Freeman at ANZ says that this is a critical aspect: 'If our staff read in the paper every other month that ... we had this debacle or were on the bottom of the pack in this measure or that measure, that's hard to take. We haven't had that; we've had great success and what staff will read about certainly from analysts and investors would be that we are well-regarded by that community for many years now'.

- How is your retention rate? ANZ notes that their turnover rate is nearly 2 percent lower than that of their peers. 'Analysts pick this stuff up nowadays. One analyst earlier this year was making comparisons about turnover, and estimated the value of the benefit that came to us each year at about 80 million dollars – that is huge', says Shane.

- How are you perceived by your customers in terms of their estimation of your internal brand? Do they perceive you to be an employer of choice?

- Do your job advertisements or your graduate intake scheme receive a lot of enquiries? ANZ takes on 300 graduates each year, and last year they received 8000 applications.

- Are your CEO and managers often sought out by the media for quotes and authoritative commentary on issues, and by organisers of conferences and other events to deliver presentations?

- Are you benchmarked by others? Shane Freeman says ANZ gets benchmarked 'by more people than we can frankly cater for'.

- Are your senior personnel consistently targeted for headhunting by other employers?

- Are your people your best recruiters? Are they Evangelists who attract their high performance friends to your organisation?

- Do you rate well in studies such as Hewitt's Best Employer? ANZ are proud to use Hewitt and say that of the ASX20, 14 use Hewitt and the ANZ score is at the top of the competitive pile of large companies in terms of staff engagement.

And the winner is…

I have spoken about a few of the top Australian performers in the Hewitt survey, but for the record, the winner for 2005 was Salesforce. Other Australian companies that won awards were:

ING Direct – best new entrant

SEEK

Swiss Re

American Express

Bain International

Bayer Healthcare ANZ

Blackmores

British American Tobacco

Carson Group

Dell Australia

Golder Associates

Medtronic

Nokia

Select Australasia

Westaff

In the 2006 Hays study of brands people would like to work for, of the 614 responses received, the top ten most frequently named ideal employers were:

1. Government/public sector

2. ANZ

3. Virgin

4. Telstra

5. Westpac

6. IBM

7. Optus

8. Microsoft

9. Vodafone

10. PricewaterhouseCoopers

How important is this to CEOs?

One of the key aspects of the fifth 'A', Assess, is to ensure that the important aspects are in fact being measured, which relates once more to the importance placed on the overall process by CEOs and senior management.

I asked all the CEOs I interviewed what differences they saw in the role of a CEO now compared with 20 years ago. Interestingly, I got quite a mixed bag of responses. There are some, quite frighteningly, who believe it is no different at all. Others note that whereas the CEO role used to be about sales, marketing and finance, a critical new factor has come to the fore, that of recruiting and retaining the best talent in order to achieve the organisation's ambitions.

The Hewitt survey suggests that an increasing number of CEOs are coming to see the importance of this issue, with over 50 percent of CEOs believing that attracting and retaining talent is one of the most important functions facing them today. Doug Shears has a refreshingly consistent approach to his people. He does not support the existence of values and mission statements, nor does he even like the concept of the employer brand. He says simply that it is about people: 'Get that right and the rest falls into place'. It's hard to argue with such straight-forward logic, not to mention some pretty sound business results by way of evidence. Graeme Wise reveals a similar attitude when he says, 'The brand isn't anything, it is nothing. It has got to be about the people'.

I guess the worrying factor is the 50 percent of CEOs who still do not see it as an issue. And when one realises that those participating in the Hewitt survey are, on average, more enlightened about people-related matters than the rest of corporate Australia, it doesn't augur well for the future.

Not to worry. 'Forced Focus' is on its way, and they'll get the message soon enough.

I hope you have found this book full of
both some challenging notions and
a wealth of ideas that will help build a
more engaged work force of the future.

10

Summary

I hope that in the course of reading this book, you have found both some challenging notions and a wealth of ideas that will help to build a more engaged workforce of the future. It feels like a journey that requires a summary of the guiding principles of employer branding, the key philosophies that will actually shape the future landscape as you seek to establish your employer brand. Here, then, are ten principles that summarise the key points you should bear in mind as you pursue your quest for a more engaged workforce.

PRINCIPLE ONE

Gen Y express their needs differently to previous generations

Plenty of people have challenged me on the nature of Gen Y, and whether or not they are really all that different to the youth of any past generation. Surely, they say, the flush of youth predisposes them towards living a footloose and fancy free existence, approaching life with gay abandon and youthful recklessness. Were we not the same in our day? Aren't all generations equally irresponsible in their youth?

I don't believe that this is the case. Certainly, there are phases in life where attitudes change dramatically, such as becoming a parent. Gen Ys will grow up and have children, and when that happens, they will go through the same reappraisal of life goals as we did, and the primal need to provide for the family will be paramount.

However, it is the way in which Gen Y will respond to that challenge that will define them, as it defined us. It is in periods of great change that the true nature of a population emerges. The characteristics Gen Y are displaying now suggest that their response will differ from that of previous generations. As noted earlier, Gen Ys are mature, certainly more sophisticated than any previous generation in the same age bracket, and very clear about what is important to them. They may appear to live a life of whimsy, but what drives their constant restlessness is the search for meaning, the desire to make a difference, and their wish to find their own version of peace and security. The way they choose to satisfy those needs will be quite different to how preceding generations sought fulfilment.

I accept that the need for security, one of the most basic of needs as identified by Maslow, is unlikely to change from one generation to the next. What I am suggesting is that the interpretation of that need is evolutionary. For my parents, security meant having a job, any job – full stop. For some Gen Ys, that definition hasn't changed, but for the opinion leaders of Gen Y, security is starting to manifest itself in a never-ending quest for self-improvement and continuous learning, a penchant for having one of every colour and style in the wardrobe so you're portable and prepared for any weather condition.

There are some characteristics of Gen Y that are sufficiently widespread to suggest distinguishable attitudinal perspectives that will become hallmarks of Gen Ys in the future, in exactly the same way that materialism defined the Baby Boomers. This will have a profound effect on every market in the future, not just the labour market.

So what does this mean for building a more engaged workforce through your employer brand? You may still be unconvinced, believing that Gen Y will eventually settle down with the wisdom of maturity and follow the same lifestyle that their predecessors did. Let's say you're right. How long do you think that will take?

In the meantime, in light of the experiences of the many employers I have spoken to who are dealing with the very real management challenges presented by Gen Y right now, the difficulty of attracting and retaining good young people, wouldn't your workplace benefit from a bit of 'Forced Focus' on this issue right now? If the world goes through another cycle, and Gen Y reverts to 'normality', then the worst that will have happened is that you've created a nicer place to work.

Would that be such a bad thing?

PRINCIPLE TWO

The labour market is cyclical – but medium term changes will be dramatic

There is no doubt that the single biggest factor affecting the labour force at present is the economic reality that, for the first time in decades, Australia is approaching full employment. The impact of this is significant, but history has taught us that it is also cyclical, and Australia's economic situation will eventually change.

So won't it all go back to 'normal' then, I hear you ask?

To be frank, who knows? I'm not an economist, so I haven't the faintest idea (nor, one might argue, have the boffins). It seems inevitable, however, that some of the trends outlined earlier in this book suggest that the evolution that is taking place will have an irrevocable effect on the future landscape. If the OECD forecast is right, and in less than ten years half of the world's workforce is concentrated in two countries, does that not suggest some fairly major effects on the world, including Australia?

Sure, Gen Ys will grow up, the world will come to grips with the increasingly aged population in developed countries, and the next generation will emerge. Meanwhile, the rate of these evolutionary changes will increase tenfold. You only need to think about the past rate of change to be able to predict the future reasonably accurately.

Peter Sheahan, in his book *Generation Y*, points out that the processor that plays 'Happy Birthday' in a $3.95 greeting card is more powerful than the processor that powered the 1976 Cray Super Computers, and has a greater capacity that that of the entire world back in 1950. It would seem that radical change is here to stay, and the principles of 'Forced Focus' will fundamentally change the future labour market landscape.

Yes, it will be cyclical change, as is the way of economics, but nonetheless it will be dramatic, and will definitely leave a legacy for future generations to grapple with.

PRINCIPLE THREE

Jobs are dead

Jobs are dead. No one wants 'em any more. Not even Baby Boomers want a job.

What we want is a life.

We want work that gives us meaning, satisfaction, control, and contentment – not just the means to an end. This is the heart of the first 'C' of Conditions. It is not merely about the functional conditions of employment anymore – it is about the experience of work, and the fulfilment it provides. No-one wants a job, but everyone wants an experience.

For those of you who are finding it so hard to manage Gen Ys in your workplace right

now, this speaks to the heart of the issue. You're looking for someone to do the job, and they're looking for an experience. The gap in the middle is obvious.

I admit I'm a little concerned about what the future may hold. The prospect of an entire generation of people who jump around frequently, don't stick it out in one career for long before changing to another, and constantly work permanent part-time in a job-share arrangement, without any one person having control of an agenda for moving forward is, quite frankly, disconcerting. I wonder about the life-skills development process. It doesn't matter what industry you are in, there are some skills that are only developed through experience – dealing with difficult individuals, building a team, learning how to prioritise, working through a complex and sensitive issue, managing stress. These are all life skills that cannot be learned in university or in jobs where tenure is consistently fleeting.

Summary ▶

And how will the art of management work in the future? We have shown an increasing tendency to flatten organisational structures, replacing traditional hierarchies with self-managed workgroups. In future, these teams will be even more multi-faceted, multi-skilled and changeable than ever, but who will manage them? What type of person will be required? Who will have the necessary expertise and training? An entirely possible scenario is a Gen X manager leading a team that is made up of one permanent part-timer, two demanding Gen Ys who want the Gen X's job, two part-time mums who are job-sharing, and a few Baby Boomers who think they're stuck doing all the work while the others are off having a life. Does that sound like an easy thing to manage? I'm pretty sure they won't be teaching that at university, either.

On the other hand, what Gen Y will produce is a range of excellent generalists – fewer specialists, but more, and better, generalists. These people will be bright, passionate and, if they are encouraged to be interested, motivated and engaged, truly loyal, rather than just habitual. They will be visionaries who do not shirk from trying something different, they will be quick to respond, they will be well-educated, street smart, and thoroughly delightful to work with. And they may well make some of the best CEOs we have ever seen.

The trick will be to understand the role that work plays in their lives. If a company can make their working life an experience, and not just a job, thereby engaging the whole person, then the workplace stands to be a more exciting, more stimulating, more fulfilling place than it has ever been.

PRINCIPLE FOUR

Consider the underemployed

While the emergence of Gen Y has been a key factor in forcing greater focus on the importance of the employer brand, they are but one labour market opportunity in a world full of talented people. When one considers the nature of the labour market, there is clearly an entire generation of people who could be utilised more in times of a skills shortage. They are wise, they are trained, they have time, they have commitment – they are the Boomers. But they too need to be spoken to differently than they have been in the past.

The principle that has emerged, whereby work should be much more about a life experience than merely a 'job' – to be able to think of work as an opportunity to be stimulated and to grow further, to enjoy a strong employer brand that makes people feel that their skills are relevant and valued, where every employee is valued for what they contribute rather than for their job title or their age – is a delicious prospect for many generations. It's a proposition to which I imagine Boomers would respond extremely positively.

The Gen Y quest of wanting to be valued and to make a difference is infectious. The entire market is moving to a different value paradigm in terms of what work means, and what people want out of their life. It is not only Gen Y who can lead the revolution. All around the world, there is a reappraisal of the value the underemployed can add, be they people with disabilities, full-time mothers, or ageing Baby Boomers. In times of short supply, good marketers exploit every possible option before they turn to alternatives and, true to the laws of 'Forced Focus', the possibility of greater choice ensures that brands must sharpen their offer in order to compete.

It is entirely likely that there is a solution for the skills shortage that is right here, right now – but not yet being utilised appropriately. The impending labour market crisis will force us to focus on that solution.

Principle Five
Not everyone is equal

As uncomfortable as this is for the socialists to accept, Pareto was right – not everyone is equal. 'Forced Focus' reflects this ethos – concentrate your efforts on those employees, customers, and stakeholders who will truly make a difference to your future.

I was lucky enough to hear a keynote address by Terry Hawkins, who paints a vivid picture of this dynamic using the analogy of a pit. She talks of the fact that three percent of the workforce are fundamentally 'pit dwellers', 'energy suckers' who suck the life out of any attempts to generate forward momentum. Her belief is that even if you continually throw ladders to pit dwellers, they will choose not to climb out of the pit. As a work colleague or manager, you cannot get them out of the pit. They must choose to get out of the pit themselves.

'Forced Focus' thinking would say that it is best to suggest they may be able to do better for themselves elsewhere. In terms of the distribution of employees between Evangelists, Uncommitted and Disengaged, the pit dwellers are the most isolated of the Disengaged, and therefore they present a learning opportunity, but do not allow your organisation to be defined by them.

They are an inevitable part of your future employer brand, but they are not the future. This goes to the first 'A', your Analysis. Understand who you want to talk to, and make sure that you get that absolutely right. Then connect with those people as best you can, so as to provide maximum meaning and engagement for the people you know have the potential and the desire to be more productively engaged and make a real difference to your future.

An engaged workforce is fundamentally different to an employed workforce.

Principle Six

The new loyalty is to people, not to the company

It was fundamentally interesting to me, as a marketing professional, to learn that the nature of brand loyalty in the employer brand market might be different to that in traditional markets. In traditional markets, the nature of brand engagement doesn't change that much. The offer might be freshened up and presented in contemporary terms, but the most successful brands have values that are generally consistent over decades.

Yet the employer brand is different. Because it is driven from the top down, it tends to take on the face of the CEO in particular. If the CEO changes, unless the brand has already been established to the degree that it is stronger than any individual, it is likely that the employer brand will also change. The influence of

a single person is an interesting dynamic. This reflects the phenomenon inherent in the fifth 'C' of Charisma – gravitation at every level towards one's immediate boss.

We used to be loyal to the companies we worked for. Now we are loyal to the people we work with.

The logical next question then is, why bother developing an employer brand at all if it is reliant on the individual? I suspect that part of the reason the individual came to the fore in the first place was because the company ceased to deliver! Once people could no longer trust the company, because it appeared that the company no longer valued them, they gravitated elsewhere. It has always been the case that one-to-one relationships are much stronger, more effective relationships than one-to-many.

So what are the implications of this? I believe they are twofold. First, I think the employer brand can still be developed and used effectively to drive loyalty if it is genuinely delivered. I look at leaders such as Andy Kennard and Peter Lancken at Kennards, Gordon Howlett at Thorn, and Doug Shears at ICM, and see that they have gone about their business without much fanfare, simply concentrating on being genuinely committed to their people. As a result, they enjoy lower than average turnover which, as was noted earlier, can be worth an awful lot. So I believe it can be done, and it seems clear that people generally

– even the infamous Gen Y – will respond to an engaging employer brand.

The second implication is that business needs to start developing leaders, not just functional experts. The building of an engaged workforce has to take place throughout the organisation, and to do this, people want to work with charismatic leaders. So you'd better make sure you've got some!

The role of the leader has always been important but, in the future, it will become critical, and serve as a key weapon in the battle to attract and retain the best people.

Principle Seven

It's not what you say and it's not how you say it. It's showing you mean it.

I have made much of the concept of 'process' in this book, which is as it should be. Process is important, because it places a structure around ideas and helps direct those who may not have innate understanding to facilitate resolutions.

However, do not mistake process for the solution itself, nor hide behind process as an excuse not to deliver. As was noted earlier, this is not a Frequent Flyer system, whereby the further you go, the more points you get. If you unveil your new employer brand with great fanfare and gusto to your ever-cynical employees, and then continue to behave exactly as you always have, it would be better not to do it at all. You are simply continuing to confirm what they've suspected all along – that you're all talk and no action, all care and no responsibility, unable to be trusted, and not worthy of the value they know they can offer. In this context, it is not better to have loved and lost than never to have loved at all.

Do them a favour. Throw this book away, ignore the five 'A's and the five 'C's, forget about articulating an employer brand, take down the mission statements and values posters that say 'we value our people', and 'we act with integrity', and do one simple thing:

Just truly value the people who work for you.

Don't say it. Don't preach it. Don't talk about it. Don't intellectualise it.

Just live it.

PRINCIPLE EIGHT

Shorten the distance between your external brand and your internal brand

Today, most companies that have an external customer face are generally aware of the importance of their brand to the balance sheet. Products are created, products are line-extended, products are diversified and products are marketed and sold. Brands emerge.

The power of the brand is undisputed and, to date, that power has been used by employers as a tool to attract employees. Working at Nike sounds like a considerably more exciting employment option than working at the local quarry. But people have begun to wise up. They've come to understand how the marketing juggernaut works so, when it comes to employment, they know to scratch below the surface and not be distracted by the sizzle.

And that's a good thing, because it keeps employers honest. Is it not a worthwhile cause to aim to have people feeling as engaged with their workplace as they do with any consumer brand to which they are loyal?

The best way to do that is shorten the distance between what the external brand stands for, and your internal brand essence. It is not just the attributes that build the brand – it is the way you go about delivering the related functional benefits that creates engagement. And so it is within the workplace. Go about your business internally as you do externally.

You might think that it's easier with a 'sexy' brand. That may well be true, but companies like Virgin Mobile and ING Direct do a great job not just because their external brand is hot, nor simply because their internal brand reflects their external brand, but because they truly believe it, they live it, they lead from the top, and they deliver the values to their people on a consistent basis.

If you force yourself to replicate the manner in which you deliver your brand essence to your external market in addressing your internal market, then your employer brand will truly resonate.

PRINCIPLE NINE

There is money to be had in getting it right

I won't dwell on this point, because it has been mentioned numerous times already, but it is a principle too fundamental to ignore. Get it right, and you will have a more productive, more engaged, more loyal and more fulfilled workforce, and that delivers cash straight to the bottom line. The cost of constantly having to find new people is only going to increase as the skills shortage develops. Focus now before you are forced to, and get ahead of the game.

Principle Ten

Force focus

People often ask me what it is about my particular style of consulting that brings the most success. I always respond that it is because I am outcomes-driven. Many consultants are happy to languish in the process, spending large amounts of time revelling in an analysis of the current and past states. I get bored with that. I like to focus on the future – to understand the past in order to help shape the future. And the key tool I use in this pursuit?

Forced Focus.

It is a way of thinking that, together with a range of tools, forces your senior management to focus, forces them to consider, and forces them to take action. As legendary US commander General George Patton said, 'A good plan violently executed now is better than a perfect plan next week'.

It may well be that the future labour force will not develop exactly as has been predicted, but there is little doubt that change is on its way, and that it will have significant implications for the future of work. Still, many people wonder – why change?

To which I respond – why not?

Why not develop a more engaged workforce? Why not maximise the opportunity for you and your employees to connect in the middle? Why not embrace the concept of work as a pursuit of a desired lifestyle, an opportunity for stimulation, a chance for people to be their best? Why not create an organisation where people really want to spend their precious time?

It is human nature to put off that which is not immediately pressing. We generally wait until we are balancing at the edge of the precipice before we decide it is time to act. I am suggesting that sometimes, the outcome can be a whole lot easier to manage if you force yourself to focus before you find yourself standing on the edge.

Acknowledgements

When reading a book, I used to give a cursory glance to the acknowledgement, looking for quirky notes about people who were important to the author. It is only now that I truly appreciate how damned important this section really is! I can quite confidently say that without this section, I wouldn't have a book.

First and foremost I need to start with my colleagues on the Defence Force Review, Avril Henry, Peter Sheahan, Mark Thomson, Flight Lieutenant Jade Hartland and Air Commodore Ken Birrer because, for me, that is where this particular journey began. Special thanks go to Peter, for planting the idea in my head to start with, for repeatedly telling me to get over myself, and for writing the outstanding Foreword. And to Avril, for her generosity of spirit, her unswerving support, and for being such a terrific role model.

The person who, other than me, probably knows this book best, is my wonderful mother Faye, who painstakingly transcribed hours and hours of taped interviews. To Mum, who never once complained, even when some of the deadlines were pretty tight, thank you so much. It would literally have been impossible without your help.

Thanks to my wonderful 'publisher', friend, mentor and fan, Lisa Messenger and her assistant, Mel. I need to bottle some of you and keep you on my desk as a permanent booster of the spirit. Thank you to my amazing Editor Geoff, who is truly a wizard with words. Thanks Stirling for the beautiful layout, and for working so hard to make this book look truly unique. I couldn't have hoped for a better outcome.

And to Alison, who worked so long and arduously on the manuscript, and who has given me so much help and support in so many ways, thank you sincerely for your terrific sense of humour, and for always being there.

Thanks Blackers for my introduction, and for encouraging me to make that fateful decision. Thanks Steve, for same.

Sincere thanks to all my friends who, when I said I was writing a book, just patiently said yes alright then, and accepted that I would be hiding under a rock for some considerable time. With only a minor warning about working too many hours from Kat, you always have my best interests at heart and I thank you all for your support.

To my incredible family, deep thanks for your support, now and always. To Michael, thanks for giving the Burke family a special appreciation of crustaceans. And to Matt, thanks for your patient and insightful comments on my manuscript.

Thanks also to all the people I interviewed for this book. To the Gen Ys, Boomers and Gen Xs, thank you for sharing your thoughts with me. Heartfelt thanks to every CEO and HR professional who spared me some of their valuable time. I appreciate you taking time out of your busy schedules to enable me to pursue my dream of writing this book.

And of course, thanks to my husband Trevor and our beautiful boys Darcy and Max. Trev, you may not have worked on the research or writing of this book, but you did more than your fair share in looking after the boys and keeping the household running so that I could keep going! I'm so lucky to have a life partner who is also my supporter, my mentor, and my best friend. All my love always.

Notations

Every effort has been made to seek approval for quoted sources. For queries please contact the publisher Essence Marketing via www.essencecomms.com.au

Note the findings of the Gallup surveys quoted on page 26 and the University of California research referred to on Page 81 are © Copyright 2004 Galt Western Personnel Ltd. You may reprint the statistics, quote from it, use it in research or projects, duplicate it or distribute it, but credit of authorship and source must be given to galtglobalreview.com.

Note Dr James McNeal who was referred to on Page 81 wrote the book *Kids Market Research: Myths and Realities* (Ithaca, NY: Paramount Market Publishing 1999).

Note the conclusions drawn from the 2003 Booz Allen and Hamilton report referred to on page 140 are entirely the author's and not those of Booz Allen and Hamilton.

Watson Wyatt Human Capital Index results on page 184 reprinted with permission from "Watson Wyatt Human Capital Index" © 2006 Watson Wyatt Worldwide. For information, visit www.watsonwyatt.com.

About Penny Burke

Penny Burke has worked in the field of advertising and marketing for over 20 years. She has lectured in marketing, has sat on numerous boards, and is the owner of Essence Communications, a marketing consultancy specialising in simplifying complex marketing issues. Penny's particular skill is bringing theoretical marketing models together with practical marketing creativity and know-how to deliver solutions that are action oriented, and deliver real outcomes and results.

Penny also facilitates a large number of workshops and strategy meetings for a range of clients. Essence has a substantial research practice that ensures Penny is talking to a whole range of everyday people about all manner of topics every week. Social research is an aspect close to Penny's heart, understanding the psychology of why people buy what they buy.

Penny is a change agent, keen to explore new boundaries and horizons and find better ways to do things. If you have any comments or suggestions regarding *Forced Focus*, please contact us at www.essencecomms.com.au.

Penny has three beautiful boys – Darcy and Max, and her husband Trev.

Index

COMING TITLES

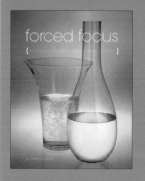

BOOK TWO –

Forced Focus; The Essence Of Facilitation From Confusion To Clarity

How often have you been involved with full-day off-site meetings that have really just been jabberfests with more questions than answers, no true team unity and no actionable outcomes achieved? The second book in the *Forced Focus* series explores the complex process of facilitation of group meetings and workshops. In *Forced Focus, The Essence Of Facilitation From Confusion To Clarity*, Penny shares some of the secrets of facilitation that applies 'Forced Focus' thinking to ensure usable and actionable outcomes. Written in the same easy style we have come to expect from Penny Burke, this *Forced Focus* book is due out **November 2007**.

BOOK THREE –

Forced Focus; The Essence Of Social Marketing

It is a well-known behavioural fact that we humans generally don't like change. Which is a problem for social marketers, because more often than not social marketing is attempting to encourage some form of behavioural change. Whether it be saving water, losing weight, driving safely or giving blood, social marketing encompasses a whole raft of behavioural change aspects for a largely unwilling populace. So how does one undertake a successful social marketing campaign? In this, Penny Burke's third *Forced Focus* book, Penny explores in detail how to deliver a well-thought-out and successful attitudinal and behavioural change campaign. Using the key aspects of 'Forced Focus' thinking to re-frame the nature of the debate in the eyes of the public, *Forced Focus; The Essence of Social Marketing* contains valuable learnings applicable to a wide range of social marketing projects. Due out **August 2008**.